Tax avoidance for
the property investor

2007-2008

indicator

ISBN 978-0-9552070-8-2

Third Edition - First print - E03P1

Introduction

Property investing has become something of a national pastime. No longer restricted to the rich and famous, everyone, it seems, wants to get into bricks and mortar. There are plenty of good reasons. For the past few years properties have grown in value faster than at any other time. Plus, with cheap, freely available finance, it's never been easier to own additional properties whether here in the UK or overseas. And with equity markets performing so badly, many people have seen their pension funds take a battering. So what better long-term alternative than an investment in property?

But of course it's not all plain sailing. Where there's an opportunity to make money, there's an opportunity for the Taxman to come along and grab a slice. So property investing means the need for some serious tax planning if you want to keep the Taxman's take to an absolute minimum.

In this book, Tax Avoidance for the Property Investor, we've considered how all the relevant taxes might come together. In plain English, we've suggested 100% legal and legitimate ways to avoid those taxes. So we've done all the hard work for you - whether you're a seasoned investor or a first-time buyer, you'll find a stack of ready-to-use tax avoidance strategies in these pages. Go ahead and try them - you've nothing to lose but a whole load of tax to save.

Duncan Callow

April 2007

Index

Section I Avoiding tax on rental income

1. Rental income - the tax basics

2. Reduce your rental income by maximising expenses

3. Making the most of your rental losses

Section II Avoiding tax on property disposals

4. Capital gains - the tax basics

5. Avoid CGT by using "Principal Private Residence" relief

6. The tax implications of gifting properties

Section III Buying strategies to avoid tax

7. Buying a property in joint names

8. Owning properties through a limited company

9. Investing in commercial property

10. Other tax considerations when buying an investment property

Section IV Overseas property tax issues

11. Moving overseas

12. Investing in overseas property

Section V Appendices

Section I

Avoiding tax on rental income

1. Rental income - the tax basics

1.1. INCOME TAX RATES

As a property investor, you have to pay income tax on the net rental income you receive on an annual basis. The amount depends on your total income for the year. The table below shows the income tax rates for 2007/8:

INCOME BAND	RATE	NOTES
£0 - £5,225	0%	No tax payable under £5,225
£5,226 - £7,455	10%	Maximum tax payable at this level of income = £223
£7,456 - £39,825	22%	Maximum tax payable at this level of income = £7,346
Over £39,825	40%	Pay 40p in every £1 of income over £39,825.

Example

Valerie receives an annual salary of £32,000 and has paid £5,623 in PAYE on this. She also has net rental profits of £8,000 for the year. Therefore, Valerie's total income is £40,000 and her total tax liability is £7,416 (£40,000 - £39,825 = £175 x 40% = £70 + £7,346). The additional tax she will have to pay on her rental income is £1,793 (£7,416 less £5,623).

Non-taxpayer

If your total income for the year, including rental income, is under £5,225 then you have no tax to pay.

Basic rate taxpayer

This is where your other income for the year is less than £39,825. Assuming rental income doesn't take you over the £39,825 threshold, it will be taxed at 22%.

Higher rate taxpayer

In this case, your other income for the year is more than £39,825. This means that your rental income will be taxed at 40%.

1.2. HOW DO I WORK OUT RENTAL PROFITS (OR LOSSES!)?

For income tax purposes, property investment is treated as a business and, therefore, net rental income is calculated in broadly the same way as self-employed business profits. To work out your net rental profits, you need to take your gross rental income in the year and subtract any ongoing, property-related expenses. See Chapter 2 for details of the expenses you can claim against income.

Example

Tina receives monthly rental income of £500 from her investment property. The property is let for the whole of the 2007/8 tax year, so she has annual rental income of £6,000. Her property-related expenses were interest on the buy-to-let mortgage of £3,600 and £80 for the annual gas safety certificate. So, Tina's taxable rental profit is £2,320 (£6,000 - (£3,600 + £80)). If Tina's other income is more than £39,825 (i.e. she is a higher rate taxpayer), then her additional tax bill will £928 (£2,320 x 40%).

1.2.1. Do I need to prepare a set of accounts?

If you own (or owned) a property and earned rent from it during the period April 6, 2007 to April 5, 2008, then you ought to prepare an income and expenditure account to establish whether or not you have made a taxable profit or loss for that year. However, these accounts do not need to be submitted to the Taxman - just keep them for your records and to help you complete your tax return.

⊙ Use the rental income calculator to prepare the accounts for you.

1.2.2. I've got two UK properties, do I need to prepare two sets of accounts?

If you have more than one UK property, then this is generally treated as a single property business. Therefore, you only need to complete one set of accounts, adding together the rental income and expenses from all the properties.

Exception: Furnished holiday accommodation

If you've got income from furnished holiday accommodation, this is taxed differently and needs to be shown separately (see 3.2 for more on the income tax treatment of furnished holiday accommodation).

Exception: Overseas property

Any overseas property that you let out needs to be shown separately from the rental income from the UK properties. Due to the different tax regimes in different countries, it is advisable to prepare one set of accounts for each country that you have properties in (see 12.2 for details of how overseas rental property is taxed).

1.2.3. Can I choose the accounting date?

The accounting period for all rental income is the tax year, i.e. April 6 to the following April 5. You can prepare accounts to a different year-end (e.g. January 1 to December 31), but the profits would then have to be apportioned to work out the profits for the year to April 5. So, unless you have strong, non-tax reasons for doing so, it would be advisable to prepare accounts to April 5 each year.

1.2.4. How long should I keep the records for?

You must keep records of your rental income and expenses for at least five years and ten months from the end of the tax year. So, your records for the year-ended April 5, 2008 need to be kept until January 31, 2014.

1.2.5. What happens if I've "lost" the records?

There's nothing to worry about, unless you have an enquiry from the Taxman. As with all tax laws, ignorance of the rules regarding the keeping of records is no excuse and, in theory, the Taxman could decide to charge a penalty for not keeping proper records. This could be up to £3,000 a year. However, this rarely happens in practice.

If, during an enquiry, you can't produce records to back up your expenses then the Taxman will use his "best judgment" and only disallow those items that he feels are incorrect. This could lead to you having to make an additional payment of tax plus interest.

1.2.6. When should I account for rental income? When it is due or when it is actually received?

The general rule is that you should account for rental income and expenses when they are due (the "accruals" basis) rather than when they are received or paid (the "cash" basis).

Exception

If your gross rental receipts are less than £15,000 a year (£1,250 a month), then you are allowed to account for rental income and expenses on a "cash" basis, i.e. when you actually receive the rent or pay the bills.

Which method should I use?

Even if your rental receipts are less than £15,000, if you receive rents in advance and pay expenses in arrears, it would be beneficial for you to account for rental income using the "accruals" basis.

> *Example*
>
> *Greg started renting a property on January 1, 2008, at a monthly rent of £800, which the tenant pays in advance. Therefore, by April 5, 2008, Greg has received four lots of £800 (£3,200). However, the last payment of £800 relates to the whole month of April. Under the "accruals" basis, Greg would include only £133 of this (£800 x 5 days/30 days) in his rental income calculation this year. If he used the "cash" basis, he would have to include the full £800. As a higher rate taxpayer, using the "accruals" basis has saved him £267 in 2007/8.*

1.3. WHICH TAX RETURNS MUST I COMPLETE IF I HAVE RENTAL INCOME?

UK property

You need to complete a self-assessment tax return that incorporates "Land and Property" supplementary pages, L1 and L2. These pages cover all types of rental income, whether it is from numerous properties or a single rental. If you have income from the commercial letting of furnished holiday accommodation in the UK then you need to complete L1. For all other UK rental income, you need to complete L2.

Overseas property

Any income from overseas land and property should not be included on the "Land and Property" pages. This income should be included on the "Foreign" supplementary pages, F4 and F5.

Jointly-held property

Each owner must include their share of the rental income and expenses on their own tax return. You do not need to complete a partnership tax return.

1.3.1. Where do I get the returns from?

If you have been sent a paper tax return without the "Land and Property" supplementary pages, you can download the additional pages from the Taxman's website (http://www.hmrc.gov.uk/sa/forms/content.htm).

If you complete your tax return online, then you can use the Taxman's free tax return software to complete the "Land and Property" pages.

1.3.2. By when do I need to submit the return?

The deadline for submission of self-assessment tax returns is January 31 following the end of the tax year. So, the tax return showing the rental income received in the year to April 5, 2008 will need to be submitted to the Taxman by January 31, 2009. There is an automatic £100 penalty for a late return.

NOTE. If you submit your return late, but have no additional tax liability, then you will avoid the automatic £100 penalty.

First-time investor

If this is the first year that you have received rental income, then, theoretically, you should advise the Taxman of your new source of income by October 5 of the following tax year. In practice, however, you won't incur any penalties as long as you submit a tax return showing the new source of income by January 31 the following year.

1.3.3. When do I pay the tax?

You need to pay any additional tax that you owe to the Taxman by January 31 following the tax year. So, for the tax year-ended April 5, 2008, you need to pay the additional tax by January 31, 2009. You will be charged interest on late payments.

If you owe more than £500 (or more than 20% of your total tax liability for the year), then as well as the additional tax, you also have to pay a further 50% on top. You then have to make another 50% payment by July 31. The two 50% payments are "payments on account" of the following tax year and will be taken off next year's tax bill.

Example

David had rental income and his additional tax liability for the year-ended April 5, 2008 was £1,500. Therefore, David has to make the following payments:

By January 31, 2009:

2007/8 tax liability	*£1,500*
2008/9 first "payment on account"	*£750 (50% of £1,500)*
Total	*£2,250*

By July 31, 2009

2008/9 second "payment on account"	*£750*

In the following tax year (2008/9), David's tax liability is £1,600.
Therefore, David will make the following payments:

By January 31, 2010

2008/9 balancing payment	*£100 (£1,600 less the two £750 "payments on account")*
2009/10 first "payment on account"	*£800*
Total	*£900*

By July 31, 2010

2009/10 second "payment on account"	*£800*

NOTE. As you can see, when you receive rental income for the first time, your initial tax bill could be substantially more than you've estimated due to the fact that you've effectively tax to pay on two years worth of profits in the first year. However, there is a way around this problem:

TIP. If your additional tax liability is less than £2,000 and you submit your tax return by September 30, this amount will be collected through your PAYE code (assuming you're employed or receiving a pension) in the following tax year.

This means that a 2007/8 underpayment will be collected by monthly instalments between April 2009 and March 2010, rather than as a single payment on January 31, 2009. This also eliminates payments on account in 2009.

1.3.4. Can I complete the returns myself or do I need an accountant?

There's no requirement to employ an accountant. However, if you have several properties, then it could be cost-effective. An accountant should charge between £250 and £750 plus VAT to complete your rental income accounts and tax return depending on the number of properties you own.

1.4. RENT-A-ROOM RELIEF

If you generate extra income by letting a room in your own home to a lodger then you can claim a special relief called "rent-a-room". Under this relief, you can earn up to £4,250 tax-free. The letting must be for residential purposes and not, for example, used as office accommodation. The lodger will typically have a furnished bedroom and share the use of other rooms.

1.4.1. Gross rent less than £4,250

If the total amount you receive in a year from letting part of your house, including charges for meals, cleaning, laundry and goods and services of a similar nature, is less than £4,250, there's no tax to pay. However, this means that if you elect for rent-a-room, any loss you make would also not be allowable.

Tip. Even if you receive rent-a-room income of less than £4,250 a year (£81 a week), make sure you add up your expenses. If they work out as more than your income, i.e. you've made a loss, elect not to apply rent-a-room for a particular year of assessment and include the rental income with your other property income. The election must be made within twelve months after the January 31 following the tax year. For example, for the 2007/8 tax year, an election must be made by January 31, 2010. You can then offset the losses against any other rental income you receive in the current or subsequent tax years.

If you want to apply the rent-a-room exemption, tick the "Yes" box on Page L1 of the tax return. If you want to elect not to apply the exemption, simply don't tick the "Yes" box! In other words, unlike some elections, you don't need to write a separate letter to the Taxman.

1.4.2. Gross rent more than £4,250

If your total rent-a-room receipts are more than £4,250, then, by default, you will be taxed on your rental income less expenses.

However, you can elect to be taxed as if the profit from the letting is equal to the difference between the total gross rents receivable and £4,250. In this case, no deduction is given for expenses.

This election must also be made within twelve months from January 31 following the end of the tax year and will continue to have effect until withdrawn. Again, it's easy to make the election - don't tick the "Yes" box on page L1 of your tax return. Instead, enter your rental income in box 5.20 and the rent-a-room exemption (£4,250) as expenses in box 5.35.

Tip. If your income is more than £4,250 and your expenses are less than £4,250, then make this election.

Example 1

Lisa lets two rooms in her house for £50 a week each (£5,200 a year). She has related expenses of £1,500, so her profit is £3,700. By default, Lisa will be taxed on her income (£5,200) less expenses (£1,500), £3,700. However, if Lisa elects to just be taxed on her rental income over £4,250, then she will only be taxed on £950 (£5,200 less £4,250) - a tax saving of up to £1,100.

Example 2

Frankie lets two rooms in her house for £80 a week each (£8,320 a year). However, she has related expenses of £4,800. By default, Frankie will be taxed on her income less expenses i.e. £3,520. If Frankie had made an election, she would have been taxed on the higher figure of £4,070 (£8,320 less £4,250).

1.4.3. Is the £4,250 per person or per property?

If you own a property jointly, the £4,250 has to be halved, i.e. £2,125 each. But it's interesting to note that the Taxman hasn't specified what happens if three or more individuals own a house in which they all live. From his guidance, it would seem that each of them has a limit of £2,125.

1.4.4. Can more than one room be let?

The rent-a-room relief applies to any proportion of the property that you live in, so renting out more than one room would qualify (as long as each room is furnished). However, the £4,250 tax-free allowance is fixed regardless of the number of rooms let out. The relief can even extend to the letting of a self-contained flat as long as the division of the property is only temporary.

1.4.5. Do I have to live in the property?

You must occupy the property as your main home at the same time as the lodger for at least part of the letting period in each tax year. This means that as long as there is an overlap between you living in the property and the lodger being there, you can move out for the rest of the tax year.

2. Reduce your rental income by maximising expenses

2.1. WHAT COSTS CAN I DEDUCT FROM MY RENTAL INCOME?

As mentioned in 1.2., as with other businesses, you are able to offset property-related expenditure against the gross rents you receive. Therefore, to reduce the amount of rental profit and, consequently, the amount of tax you pay, you need to claim as many expenses as possible. However, in order for the Taxman to allow the expenditure, it has to obey the following rules:

"Wholly and exclusively"

This means that you cannot deduct an expense that is used partly for the property and partly for another purpose UNLESS the property proportion of that "mixed" expense can be separately identified.

Example

Steve is refurbishing his own home and his investment property. He goes to a DIY store and buys ten boxes of floor tiles for £200. He uses four on his own property and six on the investment property. Therefore, he can claim 6/10ths of £200 against his rental income.

Steve also pays a cleaner £50 a week (£2,600 a year) for ten hours work. The cleaner spends two hours a week at Steve's own home and eight hours cleaning his investment properties. Therefore, Steve can deduct £2,080 (8/10ths of £2,600) against his rental income.

Paid by you

Only expenses that are actually paid by you can be offset against your rental income. For example, if it is your tenant's responsibility to pay the Council Tax and TV licence, then you cannot deduct these expenses from the rental income you receive.

Not capital

Deciding on whether costs are capital is a grey area. Even the Taxman admits it is "far from easy". Basically, costs that you incur in the day-to-day running of your property investment business are not capital expenses and can be deducted from your rental income. However, costs incurred in significantly improving your property are considered capital and cannot be deducted.

Note. Although the capital costs cannot be deducted against your rental income, they can be deducted from your sale proceeds when you sell the property (see 4.2.3.).

So as long as you can prove that the expenditure meets the above rules, you can claim it. On the following pages, we look more in depth at the typical expenses you can deduct from your rental income.

2.2. INTEREST CHARGES

Buying a property to rent out usually involves some level of borrowing. You can offset the interest paid on these loans against your rental income.

2.2.1. What is meant by interest charges?

Interest charges are the amounts you pay back to a lender which are above and beyond the initial amount that you borrowed.

2.2.2. Which types of interest can I claim?

The general rule is that you can claim interest on any loans that are incurred for the purposes of the property investment. Whether the loan interest is an allowable deduction doesn't depend on which property the loan is secured on, but rather on what the loan funds are used for.

Interest on a mortgage on the investment property

Most property investors don't have the funds to purchase properties outright. Instead, they take out a mortgage to buy the property. It doesn't matter whether the mortgage is an "interest-only" or a "repayment" mortgage. However, it's only the interest element of the mortgage repayment that can be offset against the rental income.

Example

Tony takes out an £80,000 interest-only mortgage to buy a rental property. His monthly repayments are £350. At the end of the year, the amount outstanding on the mortgage will still be £80,000 and the annual interest will be £4,200 (12 x £350). The entire £4,200 can be offset against his rental income.

Joan takes out an £80,000 repayment mortgage to buy a rental property. Her monthly repayments are £650. At the end of the year, the amount outstanding on her mortgage is £76,000 and, therefore, the annual interest is £3,800 (12 x £650 less the £4,000 reduction in the loan). In this case, Joan can only claim the £3,800 against her rental income.

Interest on a mortgage on your own home

You cannot deduct the interest on a loan taken out to buy your own property. However, if you later extend your mortgage and use the funds to purchase another property, then the interest on the extended portion can be offset against the rental income.

Example

You buy an investment property for £100,000. As with many buy-to-let mortgages, you can only borrow 80% of the purchase price. Therefore, you re-mortgaged your own home to raise the additional £20,000 deposit. The interest on the £20,000 can be claimed against the rental income.

NOTE. It's unlikely your mortgage lender will give you a separate interest statement for this, so you'll need to work out the interest on the additional loan. This is done by apportioning the loan interest:

Example

You increased your original mortgage by £20,000 to £100,000 to help buy the property and the total interest charged for the year was £6,000. The amount of interest that you can claim against your rental income is £1,200 ((£20,000/£100,000) x £6,000).

Interest on a re-mortgage

You may decide to re-mortgage the investment property (see 4.5. for more on re-mortgaging). If you re-mortgage with another lender then you can still claim the interest against your rental income. However, if you re-mortgage for a greater amount, then you can only offset the interest on the additional amount as long as it doesn't exceed the value of the property when it was first let (see example 2 in paragraph 45700 in the HMRC's Business Income Manual (http://www.hmrc.gov.uk/manuals/bimmanual/BIM45700.htm)). If the remortgage does exceed the value of the property when first let, then you can only offset interest on the additional amount if it is used solely for the investment property (or to buy another investment property).

Example

Nick buys a rental property for £160,000 with a mortgage of £128,000 and a monthly interest charge of £550. A few years later, the property value has increased to £200,000, so Nick decides to re-mortgage to

£160,000 with monthly interest of £680. He decides to use the additional £32,000 to modernise the kitchen and bathroom in the property. Nick can therefore offset the whole of the monthly interest (£680) against his rental income.

But even if Nick had decided to use the additional £32,000 to modernise the kitchen and bathroom in his own home, then he could still offset the interest. However, if Nick had re-mortgaged the property to £170,000 and used the additional funds for a private purpose, then he can only offset the proportion of the interest that relates to the loan on the initial value of the property (i.e. £160,000).

"Let and buy" mortgages

"Let and buy" is where you decide to buy a new home and let out your old one instead of selling it. Often, the mortgage on the existing property is increased to release funds to help buy the new one. In this case, the additional funds haven't been used on the existing property. So does this mean you can't claim the additional interest?

When you carry out this type of arrangement, you are effectively transferring the existing property to your "property investment business" at its market value on the date it is first let. You are also transferring the mortgage on the property at that date. Therefore, you can deduct all the let property mortgage interest against your rental income.

You can also deduct the additional interest where you further increase the mortgage on the let property as long as the borrowings are less than the market value of the property when it was first let.

Example

Helen and Mark bought their original home for £80,000 with a mortgage of £70,000. Two years later, they decide to buy a new house and let their existing property that is now worth £160,000. To get the deposit for the new house, they re-mortgage to £128,000 (80%). The interest on the full £128,000 is allowable against their rental income even though they used the extra funds to purchase their own home.

Interest on personal loans

If you take out a personal loan that is used to buy, repair or improve the property, then the interest charged on this loan can be offset against rental income.

Finance agreements

If you purchase goods for your investment property using an in-store finance agreement, then the interest is an allowable expense.

NOTE. In this case, the interest can be offset whether you use the "10% wear and tear allowance" or the "renewals" method (see 2.5.).

Interest on credit cards

The interest paid on credit cards is generally not a deductible expense when calculating interest paid. This is because it's difficult to determine which part of the outstanding balance relates to funds for the property and which relates to consumer spending. However, if you originally had a nil balance on your credit card and you only use it for buying items for your property business, then there's no reason why you shouldn't claim the monthly interest charge.

2.2.3. How do I calculate the interest on mortgages?

At least once a year, you should receive a mortgage statement or interest certificate from your mortgage lender. This will show the amount of interest paid during the last year. If it doesn't show the interest paid to April 5, you will need to ask your lender for an up-to-date statement. Your lender may make a small charge for this (this too can be included as an expense!).

2.2.4. How do I calculate the interest on personal loans and finance agreements?

Repaying a personal loan or finance agreement usually involves making a fixed monthly payment over a set number of months. These monthly payments include both capital and interest. However, it's only the interest element of the monthly repayment that you can claim against your rental income. The problem is working out how much of each instalment you pay is interest and how much is actually paying back the loan. In fact, there are two main ways to calculate the interest element and both are acceptable to the Taxman.

Straight-line method

Using this method, the interest is calculated by dividing the total interest charges by the number of months of the loan to get a monthly interest figure.

Example

You take out a three-year personal loan to refurbish the investment property for £15,000. The finance charges are £3,000. The total you will pay back is £18,000 so your monthly repayments are £500 (£18,000/36). Using the straight-line method, interest of £83.33 (£3,000/36) will be repaid each month.

Sum of digits method

This method takes into account the fact that you pay more interest at the beginning of a loan because there is more outstanding on it. You work out the number of payments you are going to make (e.g. for a three-year loan you will be making 36 monthly payments). You then work out the sum of digits (e.g. 1+2+3+4+5...+35+36 = 666 for a three year loan). The interest on the first payment is then 36/666ths of total interest payable, the interest on the second payment is 35/666ths, the third 34/666ths and so on. The interest on the final payment is 1/666th of the total interest payable.

Example

As above, you have taken out a £15,000 personal loan for the property over three years. The total interest payable is £3,000. The first month's interest will be £162.16 (£3000 x 36/666), the second month's £157.66 (£3000 x 35/666) and so on.

As you can see, the sum of digits method produces a much bigger interest figure to deduct against your rental income in the earlier years.

Tɪᴘ. Use the sum of digits method to calculate the interest you pay on fixed-rate personal loans and finance agreements so that you can get the tax relief sooner rather than later.

2.2.5. Plan your mortgage strategy

As a property investor, it is important for you to plan your mortgage strategy. As you can't get tax relief on a loan to buy your own property, aim to borrow as much as possible against your investment properties and use the additional funds generated to pay off the mortgage on your own property. That way, you will get tax relief on all your borrowings.

2.3. STRUCTURAL REPAIRS AND MAINTENANCE COSTS

The Taxman's general rule is that you can claim for any expenses that "prevent the property from deteriorating". This means that you can't offset the costs of any improvements you make to the property against your rental income. Due to the nature of property, the distinction between repairs and improvements is a grey area and causes many problems.

NOTE. Any improvement costs that you can't offset against your rental income can be offset against your capital gain when you sell the property (see 4.2.3.).

TIP. One of the requirements for expenditure to rank as capital improvements is that it should be relatively substantial and "one-off" in nature. So, if instead of spending a huge amount on a property all at once, you undertake a rolling programme of improvement, this is more likely to get allowed as a repair and therefore "revenue" expenditure.

2.3.1. Which structural costs can I claim?

You can claim the following costs against your rental income:

- exterior and interior painting
- damp and rot treatment
- replacing roof slates, flashing and gutters
- re-pointing
- mending broken windows
- stone-cleaning.

TIP. Where you are having structural work done to a property, ask the builder for a fully itemised invoice so that you can easily identify the allowable repair costs.

2.3.2. The exceptions

Insulation costs

From April 6, 2004 to April 5, 2015, you can claim the cost of new loft or cavity wall insulation of up to £1,500 per residential investment property. With effect from April 6, 2006, this allowance was extended to include draft proofing and insulation for hot water systems. And with effect from April 6, 2007 floor insulation is also included.

NOTE. This relief cannot be claimed where the property qualifies under the rent-a-room scheme or as furnished holiday accommodation. The £1,500 maximum deduction is per property and not per building. This means that a maximum of £1,500 will now be deductible for each flat in a block of flats.

Double-glazing

You can claim the cost of replacing single-glazed windows with double-glazed windows against your rental income. The Taxman has agreed that this is not an improvement, but merely a replacement with the modern equivalent.

NOTE. If the Taxman accepts that double glazing is no more than the "modern equivalent" of single-glazing, then you can argue that any structural work that replaces old materials with the "modern equivalent" can be deducted from rental income. For example, the cost of replacing wooden beams with steel girders or lead pipes with copper or plastic ones would be an allowable deduction.

2.4. RENEWING FIXTURES AND FITTINGS

Fixtures and fittings are items that are attached to the property and generally cannot be removed without causing damage to it. As a rule of thumb, they are the things that are not normally removed by the seller when a property is sold. They would include:

- radiators
- light fittings
- kitchen units
- baths, washbasins and toilets.

You can claim the cost of repairing or replacing an old or broken fixture as long as it is done on a "like-for-like" basis (i.e. with the closest modern equivalent) and not for a superior product.

2.4.1. Can I claim the costs of a new kitchen or bathroom?

Existing let property

If you want to put a new kitchen or bathroom in a property that you've already let out, whether the costs can be reclaimed depends on whether you are just replacing "like-for-like" or making improvements too. "Like-for-like" is allowable, but improvement costs are not (http://www.hmrc.gov.uk/manuals/pimmanual/PIM2020.htm).

> *Example*
>
> *Fred owns and has let out a property for the past seven years. He has now decided to replace the rather worn-out bathroom suite. The original bathroom consisted of a bath, washbasin and toilet. To refurbish the bathroom and replace the old suite on a "like-for-like" basis will cost*

£3,000. As Fred has made no "improvements", he can claim the whole £3,000 against his rental income.

If Fred decides to add a shower (costing £500) to the bathroom when he refurbishes it, then he won't be able to claim this additional cost against his rental income. However, he will be able to claim the costs against his capital gain when he sells the property.

TIP. If you are having refurbishment work done, ask for a fully itemised invoice, so you can easily separate out the capital costs.

New property not yet let

If you've purchased a property and decide to carry out refurbishment works before you let it for the first time, you cannot deduct the costs of installing or replacing the fixtures and fittings from your rental income. However, do keep the receipts for any work done, because these can be offset against your capital gain when you sell the property.

TIP. If possible, consider deferring any major refurbishments until after the property is let. The tax savings could outweigh the lower initial rent you might have to accept.

Example

You have just bought a buy-to-let property. The kitchen is functional, but needs refurbishing (but not improving!). The cost of the refurbishment is £2,000. If you rent the property before refurbishment, the market rent will be £400 a month. If you carry out the refurbishment and then rent out the property, you can get £500 a month. On a six-month short-term tenancy, as a higher rate taxpayer, you'll make an additional £360 (£600 x 60%) if you carry out the refurbishment first. However, you'll save £800 (40% of £2,000) by carrying out the refurbishment once the property is let.

2.5. RENEWING FURNITURE AND FURNISHINGS

Do not confuse furniture and furnishings with fixtures and fittings. Furniture and furnishings are effectively moveable items and include:

- beds
- sofas
- table and chairs
- curtains and carpets
- "white" goods such as a washing machine or freezer.

There are two ways that you can claim for the cost of renewing these items. You can either claim the actual cost of buying replacement furniture or you can claim a "wear and tear" allowance. You cannot claim both.

NOTE. Whatever method you choose, you cannot deduct the initial cost of furnishing a property against your rental income.

2.5.1. "Wear and tear" allowance

This is only relevant if the property is residential and let fully furnished. A furnished property, according to the Taxman, is one which is capable of normal occupation without the tenant having to provide their own beds, chairs, tables, sofas and other furnishings. If you provide only nominal furnishings, the property will not meet the test, and you can't claim the allowance.

TIP. Make sure you rent the property with just enough furniture to qualify as fully furnished so that you can claim the wear and tear allowance. The cost of second-hand furniture is very low compared to the tax savings you could make.

The allowance is calculated by taking 10% of the rents received after deducting any charges for services paid by you that would normally be the tenant's responsibility (e.g. water rates and Council Tax).

> *Example*
>
> *Martin rents out a fully furnished property for £750 a month (£9,000 a year) inclusive of water rates and Council Tax. He pays out £200 a year for water rates and £1,000 for Council Tax. He can claim a wear and tear allowance for the year of £780 (10% of (£9,000 - £1,200)). This gives a tax saving of up to £312.*

2.5.2. "Renewals" basis

Instead of the "wear and tear" allowance, you can claim the net cost of replacing a particular item of furniture etc. with the proviso that no relief has been claimed on the original purchase. The net cost means that you must deduct any income you receive from the sale of the old item of furniture from the purchase cost of the replacement item.

2.5.3. Which method should I use?

The wear and tear allowance is very generous and will, therefore, usually work out to be more beneficial than claiming the actual cost of replacement furniture. Also, you can start claiming the allowance as soon as you have rental income rather than wait until you replace furniture at some point in the future.

2.5.4. Can I use a different method for different properties?

Unfortunately, no. Once you have chosen a method, you have to use it on all your let furnished properties. So, if you decide to claim the wear and tear allowance, you will never be able to claim the cost of replacing furnishings.

Tip. If you do own two properties and you've worked out that it's preferable to claim the wear and tear allowance for one and the renewals basis for another, then you could consider transferring one property to your spouse so that you can each claim the most beneficial method.

2.5.5. If I claim wear and tear, will I still be able to claim the cost of repairing fixtures and fittings?

Yes you can. The wear and tear rule only applies to furnishings so a claim for the cost of repairs to fixtures and fittings (see 2.4) would be allowed.

2.6. CAPITAL ALLOWANCES

As a landlord, you may have had to purchase equipment and machinery "wholly and exclusively" (see 2.1) for managing your properties. You may have bought office equipment, such as a computer, which you just use to keep your rental records. You may also own machinery for maintenance of the properties, such as a carpet washer or a drill. As these items are likely to last for more than one year, you can't claim the full purchase cost against your rental income in the year you buy them. However, you are allowed to claim a percentage of the cost and this percentage is known as a "capital allowance".

2.6.1. What percentage of the cost can I claim?

For equipment bought in the tax years to April 5, 2007 and April 5, 2008, you can claim 50% of the purchase cost. In the years following the year you bought the equipment, you can claim 25% of the remaining cost (known as the "written down value").

Example

David owns two investment properties. In June 2006, he purchases a carpet washer for £200 to clean the carpets between lettings. David can claim for the cost of the carpet washer as follows:

Tax year	Cost less already claimed	% claim	Amount claimed
2006/7	£200	50%	£100
2007/8	£100	25%	£25
2008/9	£75	25%	£19
2009/10	£56	25%	£14 etc.

NOTE. You cannot claim capital allowances on equipment or furniture inside a residential property. This is because you can claim the wear and tear allowance or the renewal cost instead (see 2.5.).

2.7. TRAVELLING COSTS

You can claim the cost of travelling to your investment property for:

- rent collection
- carrying out maintenance and repairs
- viewings with prospective tenants.

2.7.1. How much can I claim?

If you are travelling by car, you can either claim a proportion of the actual running costs or a fixed amount per mile.

Actual running costs

If you are using this method, then you should keep a diary of the dates and reasons you travelled to the property. You will also need to know:

- the mileage between your home and the property (it's quite acceptable to use an internet-based route-finder to work this out)
- the total number of miles your car has done in a year (from its service record or MOT certificate)
- the annual running costs of your car (fuel, road tax, insurance, repairs and servicing).

First of all, you calculate the percentage of property business miles you have done compared with total miles for the year. You can then deduct this percentage of the running costs against your rental income. You can also deduct the same percentage of your car's capital allowance. In the first year it is claimed, the maximum capital allowance for a car is the lower of 25% of its market value (at the start of the tax year) or cost (if bought in tax year) and £3,000. In subsequent years, the capital allowance will either be 25% of the "written down value" or £3,000.

Example

Hugh lives in London and visits his investment property in Leeds once a month to collect the rent and carry out any essential repairs. The journey is 200 miles each way, so he does 4,800 property business miles in a year. Hugh's total mileage for the year is 12,000 miles. Therefore, Hugh can claim 40% (4,800/12,000) of his car running costs against his rental income:

RUNNING COST	COST	40% CLAIM
Petrol	£1,000	£400
Road tax	£165	£66
Servicing	£300	£120
Insurance	£350	£140
Total	**£1,815**	**£726**

The current market value of his car (according to Glass's guide) is £9,000. The total capital allowance would therefore be 25% of this, £2,250. However, he can only claim 40% of this i.e. £900. So, in total, he can deduct travelling expenses of £1,626. As a higher rate taxpayer, this will save him £650 in tax.

Fixed amount per mile

Rather than claiming actual costs, a much simpler method is to claim a mileage allowance. You can claim a tax-free mileage allowance of 40p per mile for the first 10,000 business miles in the tax year and then 25p after that. You still need to keep a diary of the dates and reasons you travelled to the property, but you don't have to worry about keeping a record of all the costs or calculating the capital allowance.

Example

Taking the above example, Hugh has done 4,800 business miles. Using the 40p per mile mileage allowance, he can claim £1,920 (4,800 miles x 40p) against his rental income. In this case, he will save £768 in tax.

2.7.2. Which method should I use?

As the examples show, assuming you do less than 10,000 miles a year visiting your properties, then claiming 40p per mile should save you more in tax than claiming for actual costs. It is also much simpler to calculate.

2.7.3. How do I split the travelling expenses when I own the property with my spouse?

Joint owners can each claim their travelling expenses separately. It doesn't have to be split 50:50. It's a good idea to have the car in the name of the higher rate taxpayer so that the motoring costs can then be offset fully against their share of the rental income and get the maximum tax relief.

2.8. PRE-LETTING EXPENSES

You may have incurred expenses before letting a property. The general rule is that you can claim expenses (as long as they would qualify under normal rules, i.e. revenue expenses) incurred in the seven years before you started renting your first property. The expenses are treated as incurred on the first day that you rented a property. Examples of costs that can be claimed are:

- advertising costs incurred when searching for tenants
- telephone calls to arrange for tenants to view the property
- travel expenses incurred to show tenants around the property.

2.8.1. Can I claim the cost of mortgage interest incurred before I let the property for the first time?

As long as you are genuinely trying to let the property but it is empty because you can't find a tenant, then you can deduct the mortgage interest. Keep copies of any ads for tenants or correspondence with letting agents as evidence of this.

2.8.2. Can I deduct the cost of "doing up" the property before it's let for the first time?

Unfortunately not. As discussed in 2.4.1., the costs of any refurbishments carried out before the property is let for the first time are generally not allowable expenses against your rental income. These costs are treated as capital costs and will be added to your purchase cost when you come to sell the property.

2.9. LEGAL AND PROFESSIONAL COSTS

You can claim all the legal and professional fees you incur in the day-to-day running of your rental business. You cannot deduct any legal fees you incur with regard to capital expenditure e.g. buying or selling the property.

So, you can claim any fees you incur in relation to the following matters against your rental income:

- obtaining a valuation for insurance purposes
- negotiation of rent reviews
- collection of rent (debt collectors)
- property management company fees (where you use a management company to manage the rental property for you)
- evicting a tenant in order to re-let the property
- accountancy fees in preparing the letting business accounts and rental tax liability
- drawing up a new tenancy agreement that is for less than one year
- renewing a lease (as long as the lease is for less than 50 years).

Unfortunately, you can't claim the fees you incur for the following matters (although you will be able to claim them against your capital gain when you sell the property):

- purchasing or selling a property
- evicting a tenant and not intending to re-let
- architects' and surveyors' fees, etc., in improving a property
- drawing up a new tenancy agreement that is for more than one year
- planning applications (unless, for example, to carry out repairs where listed building consent is required).

2.9.1. Can I claim my accountant's fees for completing my personal tax return?

Although you can claim your accountant's fees for preparing your rental accounts, theoretically, you can't claim their fees for preparing your personal tax return. In practice, this is very rarely challenged by the Taxman. To be on the safe side, there shouldn't be any "confusing" words on your accountant's invoice i.e. it should just refer to "the completion of your rental accounts and calculation of the tax liability".

2.10. COSTS OF SERVICES PROVIDED, INCLUDING WAGES

In order to keep your rental property in good condition, you may pay for the services of a cleaner or gardener and these costs are fully allowable against your income. It is best to pay them by cheque so that you have a record of the payments. If you do pay them in cash, make sure you get some form of receipt to back up your claim.

It's absolutely fine to use the same person who cleans your own home or does your garden. However, if you pay them a total weekly amount of, say, £50, you should only claim the amount that relates to cleaning the rented property.

2.10.1. Can I claim the cost of paying my spouse/ partner a wage for managing the property?

Yes, you can pay your spouse or partner a wage for dealing with the administration of the let properties as long as they don't own part of the property. In fact, this is a good way for them to receive some income from the property without you having to give them a share in it. Their duties could include finding tenants, arranging inventories, check ins/outs, dealing with tenant queries and preparing the rental accounts etc.

2.10.2. How much can I pay them?

The Taxman says you have to pay them "a proper commercial reward" for the work they do. For a commercial rate per hour, have a look at what a managing agent would charge you and then discount this by 50% for a non-specialist putting the hours in. However, you mustn't pay less than the National Minimum Wage, currently £5.35 per hour (but rising to £5.52 per hour on October 1, 2007). It's likely that a managing agent would charge a fee of at least £15 an hour, so you could pay £7.50. If you can justify just two hours work a week for 48 weeks a year, you could pay a salary of £720 for the year. As a higher rate taxpayer, this would save you £288 in tax and as long as their total income for the year (2007/8) is less than £5,225, they won't pay any tax.

NOTE. The salary should not be set at a level which will result in the letting business making a loss. Otherwise, the Taxman will not allow you to use that part of the loss.

TIP. Rather than put your spouse's wages in box 5.28 "Costs of services provided, including wages", put them in box 5.27 "Legal and professional costs" as they are "management fees for the on-going costs of letting". By doing this, you are less likely to draw the attention of the Taxman (or his computer!) and get an unnecessary enquiry.

2.11. OTHER EXPENSES

<u>Gas safety inspection</u>

As a landlord, you are required by law to have an annual safety inspection of all gas appliances. The inspection has to be carried out by a CORGI registered engineer who will then give you a gas safety certificate. You can claim for the cost of obtaining the certificate.

<u>Advertising costs</u>

If you advertise for tenants in newspapers or magazines, you can offset the costs of the ads against your rental income.

If you pay to register your property for letting on a website, you can also offset the cost against your rental income.

You cannot offset the costs of advertising your property for sale - this is a capital cost and can be offset against your capital gain (see 4.2.4.).

<u>Magazines and books</u>

You can offset the cost of any magazines or books for the purposes of your property business e.g. this book! Just make sure it satisfies the "wholly and exclusively" rule. For example, it may be difficult to claim for the costs of interior design magazines every month if you only redecorate a property once every five years.

<u>Property seminar costs</u>

Over the past few years, as the interest in property investment has increased, there has also been a steady increase in companies offering property investment seminars. Typically, these seminars cost several thousand pounds, so it would be nice to be able to deduct them from your rental income.

If you're already a property investor and attend a course to refresh your investment skills, then you can offset the entire cost, as you will be regarded as updating your skills.

However, if you're thinking of investing in property for the first time and attend a course to explain how to do this, then you will not be able to offset the costs against the rental income. This is because you will not just be "updating your skills", you will be learning new ones.

TAXMAN WARNING! Having large seminar costs in box 5.29 "Other expenses" could trigger an investigation. If you have had an investment business for a few years and are just updating your knowledge, then include the breakdown of other expenses in the white space on your tax return.

Telephone

You can claim the cost of any telephone calls you make with regard to your property business such as those to a letting agent or tenant. You will need to keep a log of these calls.

TIP. Check whether your phone company allows you to split your telephone bill into two sections by entering a code before dialling the number. That way you can have one code for property business calls and another for personal calls and they will be shown separately on the bill.

If you have a dedicated phone line for your property business or a separate mobile phone, then you can also claim the cost of any line rental.

Use of home as office

Like most property investors, you probably manage your let properties from home. So, can you claim part of the general running costs of your home against your rental income? Well, you might have thought that because expenses must be incurred "wholly and exclusively" you wouldn't get any relief. However, in practice, the Taxman agrees that where there is part-business and part-private use of a home, the running costs can be apportioned.

If you do have a separate study/office to run your property business, then you can claim a share of your home running costs based on the proportion of the room in relation to your whole house. This is supposed to be done on a "floor area" basis, but in practice, the Taxman allows a proportion based on the number of rooms in a house. For example, if you have twelve rooms in your house and one of them is dedicated to your property business, then you can deduct 1/12th of your running costs. Allowable running costs include Council Tax (or rates), water rates, mortgage interest and buildings and contents insurance. Heating and lighting costs can be apportioned on the same basis, though it may be that the facts support apportioning a larger amount to the office on the basis of usage. After all, the computer is on all day. And if an office or study has been built specifically for the business, there is no reason why interest on any loan taken out to finance the building work should not be deductible in full.

However, if "working from home" involves little more than setting papers out on a corner of the dining-room table for a few hours a month, then you may find it hard to convince the Taxman that you've incurred additional costs.

If your spare bedroom doubles as an office during the week and guest accommodation at the weekend then you need to apportion the total running costs first on the basis of floor area (or number of rooms). The part relating to the room should then be apportioned by reference to the time it is used for domestic or rental business purposes e.g. 5/7ths.

TAXMAN WARNING! If you use a room in your own home exclusively for business, then the Taxman may disallow a proportion of the Principal Private Residence relief (see 5.1) when you com to sell the property. The way round this is simply to make sure that the room is used for both private and business purposes.

3. Making the most of your rental losses

3.1. WHAT IS A RENTAL LOSS?

You will incur a rental loss if the expenses you claim against your rental income are greater than the rent you receive. The treatment of losses is different depending on whether you have general UK property, furnished holiday accommodation (see 3.2.) or overseas property. Losses on overseas property will be dealt with in 12.2.5.

3.1.1. What can I do with a loss on general UK property?

<u>More than one property</u>

If you have several properties, then any loss you make on one is automatically set off against the profits from the others, in the same year. This is because the income from all your UK properties (except furnished holiday accommodation) is treated as a single property "business" (see 1.2.2.).

<u>Overall net loss</u>

If the rental profits from other properties don't cover the whole loss, or you don't own any other properties, then you can carry the loss forward and set it against your rental income of the following tax years until it is used up.

> *Example*
>
> *In the tax year ending April 5, 2008, Angie received rental income of £5,000. However, her total property expenses were £6,000, so she made a £1,000 loss and had no tax to pay. In the following tax year, Angie receives rent of £6,000 and pays out £4,000 in expenses. Therefore, she has made a profit of £2,000. Angie must offset the previous year's loss of £1,000 against this. So, although she's made a profit of £2,000, she's only taxed on £1,000 of it.*

3.1.2. How do I claim the loss?

You don't need to write a separate letter to the Taxman to claim the loss. On the second "Land and Property" page, enter the amount of the loss to carry forward in box 5.45 "Loss to carry forward to the following year".

3.1.3. Can I offset losses from a previous property against income from one bought several years later?

If you stop investing in property for several years and then start again, you could be classed as ceasing one business and starting up another. Therefore, theoretically, the rental losses would disappear when the first source of rental income stops.

<u>What was your intention?</u>

However, if it was your intention when selling the old investment property to purchase another one and let it out, then even though you didn't do so until several years later, you have a strong argument (backed up by case law - Kirk & Randall Ltd v. Dunn) for carrying the loss forward and setting it off against the profits arising on the new property. As always, the challenge is in convincing the Taxman that it was your intention. Therefore, to strengthen your case, make sure you keep a record of all the potential investment properties you looked at prior to buying the second property (take pictures), correspondence with estate agents and dates you visited property auctions etc.

3.1.4. Can I offset the loss against my other income in the year?

Generally, no. Although rental profits and losses are calculated in much the same way as self-employed businesses, the treatment of losses is different. Unlike self-employed business losses, rental losses cannot be offset against the other income of the taxpayer. However, there are two notable exceptions: losses on furnished holiday accommodation (see 3.2) and excess capital allowances.

<u>Exception - excess capital allowances claimed</u>

As discussed in 2.6., if you let residential property, you can claim "capital allowances" for certain equipment you use in your property business (as long as it's not kept inside the let property). If you own and let out commercial property (including furnished holiday accommodation) then you have even more opportunity to claim capital allowances (see 9.5.).

So, if you have claimed capital allowances against your rental income in calculating the loss, then you can make a claim to offset these capital allowances against your other income in the year of the loss (or the following year) instead. The advantage of this is that you will get tax relief for part of the loss now, rather than in some future tax year. The capital allowances you offset must not exceed your rental loss.

> *Example*
>
> *Frank makes a business loss of £1,000 in the year ended April 5, 2008. Included in his property expenses are capital allowances of £900 relating to equipment he bought to run his letting business.*
>
> *Frank can make a claim to offset the £900 capital allowances against his other income in the year to April 5, 2008. The remaining £100 of the loss will be carried forward and set against future profits from his letting business. If Frank is a higher-rate taxpayer, he will make a tax saving in 2007/8 of £360.*
>
> *If Frank's capital allowances had been £1,100, he could only have offset a maximum of £1,000 against his other income as he can't offset more than the loss.*

To make the claim, enter the amount of the capital allowances in box 5.44 on the "Land and Property" pages. This claim must be made within twelve months of the January 31 filing deadline. So, a claim for the year ended April 5, 2008 would have to be made by January 31, 2010. This means that even if you've already submitted your tax return, you can make a claim to change it by sending the Taxman amended "Land and Property" pages with box 5.44 completed.

3.1.5. Can I let a property to a relative for a nominal rent and still claim all my property related expenses?

Yes, you can. The only problem is that as the letting is not on a "commercial" basis, the Taxman will not allow you to offset the loss against the rental profits of any other properties. In fact, all you can do with the loss is carry it forward and offset it against any future profits you make on the same letting (i.e. the same tenant at the same property). Therefore, there's no real tax advantage in making a loss on a non-commercially let property.

3.1.6. If I always make losses on my rental property, do I need to declare them to the Taxman?

As mentioned in 1.3.2., in theory, you should let the Taxman know that you have a new source of income by October 5 of the following tax year.

However, in practice, as long as you complete a tax return by January 31 of the following year showing the new source of income, you won't incur a penalty.

Obviously, the Taxman won't necessarily find out if you don't tell him about your new source of income. However, if you don't declare the losses and then you begin to make profits in later years, you won't be able to offset any of these losses against the future profits. Therefore, you may end up paying more tax than you would if you had declared the losses in the first place.

3.2. FURNISHED HOLIDAY HOMES

Letting property is treated as a business; however, it is not treated as a "trade". This means that your net rental income is not considered "earned" income. However, there is an exception. If you invest in and let a UK property that qualifies as a "furnished holiday home", then it will be treated as "earned" income and will therefore benefit from some attractive income tax rules:

- your net income from holiday lets counts as part of your earnings for pension contributions

- you can claim capital allowances on any money spent on furnishings and equipment for the holiday home (this isn't available to most residential accommodation - see 2.6.)

- if you make a loss on your holiday let(s), you can offset it against your other income in the year (see 3.2.3.) and claim a tax rebate. There is no relief against general income for losses arising from any other kind of letting.

NOTE. Although it is treated as earned income, there's no need to pay Class 4 National Insurance contributions.

There are also significant Capital Gains Tax advantages which are discussed in 6.2.

3.2.1. Does my property qualify as a "furnished holiday home"?

With such appealing tax advantages on offer, you won't be surprised to learn that there are strict qualifying criteria:

- the accommodation must include some furniture

- it must be available for commercial letting (see 3.2.2.) to the public generally (i.e. not your family!), as furnished holiday accommodation, for at least 140 days (20 weeks) a year; and

- it must actually be let for at least 70 days (ten weeks) a year; and

- in any period of at least seven months, the property should not normally be let to the same person for more than a month (technically 31 days) at a time; and

- the property must be in the UK - overseas holiday homes don't qualify.

NOTE. If you've let more than one furnished holiday home then you don't have to let out both properties for 70 days each as long as the average is 70 days or more. So, if you had two properties, one could be let for 60 days and another for 80 days.

TIP. Make sure you keep your booking diary showing the names and addresses of the holidaymakers together with the dates of their stay. This will provide proof to the Taxman, if required.

3.2.2. What does the Taxman view as "commercial letting"?

As the reliefs for qualifying holiday lets are so generous, the Taxman will look very closely at them. In particular, he will want to see that you have set up the holiday letting business in order to make profits. Therefore, if your main motive is to buy a second home (perhaps for retirement), then the Taxman may disallow it as a holiday home even though you fulfil the other criteria. Also, the letting is very unlikely to qualify if the interest on any loan you take out to buy the property is always more than the rental income.

This doesn't mean you're expected to make a profit on your holiday home from day one, but the Taxman would expect to see the holiday home business being profitable within five years of starting.

TIP. In order to establish, if need be at a later date, that the letting is on a "commercial" basis, produce a spreadsheet showing the income you expect to be generated from it over the next five years and the related expenses (which must be less!). In particular, make sure the annual mortgage interest is less than the expected rental income.

3.2.3. What can I do with a loss on furnished holiday accommodation?

Offset against other income

As mentioned in 3.2., if you do make a loss on your holiday let, you can offset it against your other income either in the tax year of the loss or the year before.

Example

Helen has a furnished holiday property and in the tax year to April 5, 2008, she has made a loss of £1,000. Her other income for the year from her employment is £25,000. Helen can offset the £1,000 loss against her employment income. As she's already paid basic rate tax on her employment income, she will receive a tax rebate of £220 (£1,000 x 22%).

In the previous tax year to April 5, 2007, Helen had employment income of £40,000. Instead of offsetting the loss against her income in 2007/8, she decided to claim it against her 2006/7 income. In this case, she will receive a tax rebate of £400 (£1,000 x 40%) because she was a higher rate taxpayer in 2006/7.

TIP. If you make a loss from your holiday home, compare the tax rates on your income in the year of the loss with your income from the year before. Offset the loss against the year when you were subject to the higher tax rate to get the maximum tax rebate.

Offset against other property income

If you've other property income, then any holiday letting losses that you choose not to use against your other income must be used to reduce this income in the same tax year.

Carry forward

If you choose not to offset the loss against your general income and you can't use it all against your other property income, then all you can do is carry it forward and offset it against the first available future profits you make on your holiday lettings.

3.2.4. How do I make the claim to deduct the loss from the previous year's income?

You need to write to the Taxman within 22 months of the end of the tax year. See Appendix A for a sample claim letter.

Section II

Avoiding tax on property disposals

4. Capital gains - the tax basics

4.1. WHAT IS CAPITAL GAINS TAX?

At some point in the future, it's likely that you will want to sell your investment property. If you're resident in the UK for tax purposes, Capital Gains Tax (CGT) is the tax that you have to pay on any capital gain (essentially the difference between what you paid for it and what you sold it for) you make on the sale. So, if your investment property has increased in value, it's likely you will have a taxable capital gain. If you're a higher rate taxpayer, this could reduce your return on investment by up to 40%.

4.1.1. Do I have to pay CGT?

If you are resident (or ordinarily resident) in the UK, you will be liable to CGT on the sale of your UK property. Companies do not pay CGT, but instead pay Corporation Tax on their capital gains.

4.1.2. What's the rate of CGT?

As with income tax, how much CGT you pay depends on your overall income. Your total taxable gains are added to your taxable income for the year and treated as the top part of that total. CGT is then charged on the gains at the following rates (2007/8 tax year):

- 10% if you earn less than the starting rate limit for income tax (£2,230)
- 20% if you earn between the starting rate and basic rate limits for income tax (£2,231 to £34,600)
- 40% if you earn more than the basic rate limit for income tax (£34,600 and above).

Therefore, if you're already a higher rate taxpayer, you will pay 40% on your gain.

NOTE. The basic rate for CGT is 20%, and not 22% as it is with income tax.

4.1.3. Can I avoid CGT by just giving the property away?

Unfortunately, as a general rule, no! If you decide to transfer or gift your property to someone else, then you will be deemed to have sold the property at the market value on the date of the gift. This means that you could end up with a tax bill even though you haven't received any sale proceeds. However, there are ways of getting around this rule and avoiding CGT when transferring or gifting certain property - see Chapter 6.

4.1.4. Are there special rules for spouses?

Yes. For CGT purposes, spouses are treated as one person. If you transfer a property to your spouse or civil partner, there is no CGT to pay. However, if your spouse eventually sells the property, the capital gain will be calculated based on the original cost and not the value when the property was transferred.

4.1.5. How much is the annual CGT allowance?

For 2007/8, each individual has an annual CGT exemption of £9,200. This means that you won't pay any CGT unless your total taxable gains in a tax year are more than £9,200.

Example

Lynn, a higher rate taxpayer, has made a taxable gain of £50,000 on her investment property. She has no other gains for the year, so she can reduce this gain by the £9,200 annual exemption. She will, therefore, pay tax on only £40,800 of the gain.

Tip. A husband and wife (or civil partners) each get their own separate exemption, so transfer the property into joint names with your spouse to double your tax-free gains to £18,400 and save additional tax of up to £3,680. See 7.2. to find out how transfer part of the property to your spouse.

Note. If you have no other income in the year, then the maximum exemption is still £9,200 i.e. you can't offset the £5,225 income tax personal allowance as well.

4.1.6. Which tax returns do I need to complete for capital gains?

You need to complete the "Capital Gains" supplementary pages for the tax year (April 6 to April 5) in which you made the gain if:

- the proceeds are more than four times the annual exemption (i.e. more than £36,800 for 2007/8) or
- CGT is due on the gain.

As it's likely that you will sell your property for more than £36,800, you will need to complete the "Capital Gains" pages whether you have to pay CGT on the gain or not. The only exception is where the gain is completely covered by the Principal Private Residence exemption (see 5.1.).

So, if you made a gain in July 2007, you will need to include the "Capital Gains" pages in your 2007/8 tax return, which needs to be submitted to the Taxman by January 31, 2009.

If you have been sent a paper tax return without these supplementary pages, you can download them from the Taxman's website (http://www. hmrc.gov.uk).

4.1.7. When do I have to pay the tax?

As the capital gains are shown on your self-assessment tax return, you need to pay the tax by January 31 following the tax year. So, the tax on gains in the year to April 5, 2008 has to be paid by January 31, 2009.

4.1.8. What's the date of sale; when we exchange contracts or when we complete?

For CGT purposes, the date of disposal is the date of the contract. Therefore, it's normally the date of exchange and not the date of completion. This is extremely important when a sale takes place around April 5.

Example

Pauline exchanges contracts on March 1, 2007 but completion doesn't take place until April 10, 2007. Pauline mistakenly thinks that she can claim that the sale took place in the tax year 2007/8, so that the tax isn't payable until January 31, 2009, 21 months later. This is entirely wrong. The sale actually took place on March 1, 2007 in the tax year 2006/7, meaning that the tax is due by January 31, 2008, only ten months later. If the Taxman discovers the error, Pauline will be charged interest from the date when the tax should have been paid. She may also incur penalties.

Tip. If you want to delay the paying of the CGT by twelve months, ask your solicitor to delay the exchange of contracts until after April 5. That way, the gain will fall into the following tax year so any tax payable is due by January 31 a year later.

4.1.9. How do I calculate the capital gain?

This is not particularly straightforward, but simply, the capital gain is calculated by taking the selling price and deducting (in the following order):

- allowable costs (see 4.2.) plus indexation relief (see 4.3.)
- any other relevant reliefs (such as principal private residence relief)
- allowable losses (see 4.6.)
- taper relief (4.4.)
- the annual exemption (see 4.1.5.).

⊙ Use the CGT calculator to work out the capital gain on your property and the potential tax liability.

4.2. REDUCE THE GAIN BY CLAIMING ALL ALLOWABLE COSTS

When working out the gain, the first thing to do is add up all the costs you incurred during the purchase and sale of the property. Then, add the purchase costs to the basic buying price and deduct the selling costs from the sale price. The idea is to maximise the purchase price and minimise the selling price so that the difference between the two (i.e. your gain) is reduced as much as possible.

4.2.1. Buying costs

Add onto your purchase price any costs that you incurred in order to buy the property. Typical costs include:

- survey fees
- solicitors' fees
- Stamp Duty Land Tax.

NOTE. As a rule of thumb, all the costs on the completion statement from your solicitor will be allowable (so make sure you keep a copy with your tax documents).

4.2.2. Travelling expenses

Your property may not be near where you live. In this case, you can quite legitimately claim the costs you may have originally incurred in travelling around the area viewing various properties before deciding to purchase. Remember not to include the costs of visiting the property to collect rent or carry out repairs, as these costs should be offset against your rental income (see 2.7.). Again, add these travel costs onto your purchase price.

Tıp. Rather than claiming actual costs, a much simpler method is to claim a mileage allowance. You can claim a tax-free mileage allowance of 40p for the first 10,000 business miles and then 25p after that. Keep a diary of the dates you travelled to the various prospective properties just in case the Taxman queries your claim.

4.2.3. Enhancement costs

If you previously let the property, then you weren't able to offset the costs of any improvements (i.e. capital costs) against your rental income (see 2.3.). However, you can deduct these costs from the sale proceeds as long as the enhancements are still there when you sell the property, i.e. they are permanent improvements. For example, you can claim the cost of adding a conservatory, loft extension or improving the kitchen. So, always keep the receipts for any improvement work you've had done.

Tıp. If you couldn't offset the costs against your rental income then you will usually be able to offset them against your capital gain when you sell the property. This includes the costs of repairs (including decorating) that were necessary before the property was let for the first time. When your annual rental accounts are prepared, keep a list of all disallowed expenditure. This list can then be reviewed when you sell the property, so that no items of expenditure are missed.

4.2.4. Selling costs

Deduct any costs incurred when selling the property from your selling price. Such costs include:

- solicitors' fees
- advertising costs
- estate agent's commission
- travelling costs - associated with selling the property such as being there for viewings with potential buyers or meeting with local estate agents. Again, you can claim 40p per mile for the first 10,000 miles and 25p thereafter.

4.2.5. Can I deduct the mortgage early redemption penalty?

Unfortunately, if you are redeeming a mortgage early, you can't deduct any early redemption penalty from your selling price. But although you cannot deduct it from your capital gain, you may be able to argue that it is a final interest payment (check the mortgage deed) and therefore offset it against any rental income in the tax year.

4.3. INDEXATION RELIEF

This relief will only apply if you purchased or acquired the property before April 1998. This relief increases the cost of the property to take account of inflation and therefore reduces your gain.

4.3.1. How do I calculate indexation relief?

This relief is based on the percentage increase in the Retail Price Index (RPI) from the date you purchased or acquired the asset (or March 1982 if later - see 4.3.3.) up to April 1998. The relevant monthly relief percentages ("indexation factors") from March 1982 to April 1998 are shown in Appendix B.

The relief is calculated by multiplying the purchase cost of the property by the indexation factor for the month that you bought (or acquired) the property.

> *Purchase cost x indexation factor for month of purchase*
> *= indexation relief*

Example

Bob bought a property in August 1992 for £50,000. He sold it in April 2000 for £70,000. The indexation factor for August 1992 is 0.171. Therefore, Bob can reduce his gain by indexation relief of £8,550 (£50,000 x 0.171).

Improvement costs

You can also claim the relief on the costs of any improvements you've made to the property. Check the dates on the receipts to find out which month you incurred the costs, find the indexation factor for that month in Appendix B and then multiply the cost by that indexation factor.

Example

Taking the above example, Bob spent £10,000 on a loft extension for the property in March 1995. The indexation factor for March 1995 is 0.102. Therefore, Bob can further reduce his gain by indexation relief of £1,020 (£10,000 x 0.102).

4.3.2. What happens if the relief is more than the gain?

Indexation relief can only be used to reduce or eliminate a capital gain. This means that the relief can't be more than the gain i.e. you can't use it to make a capital loss.

> *Example*
>
> *Taking the first example above, if Bob sold the property for £58,000, he has only made a gain before indexation of £8,000. In this case, the maximum amount of indexation relief that he could offset would be £8,000 (and not £8,550).*

4.3.3. I purchased the property before March 31, 1982, so what indexation factor do I use?

This relief was only introduced in March 1982, so indexation factors only start from that date. However, if you bought or acquired a property before that date, then the "purchase cost" for the calculation is the higher of the actual purchase cost and its market value at March 31, 1982. In practice, if you don't know its market value at that date then you could use the purchase cost. However, using the market value in the calculation will probably save you more tax, as it's likely to be higher than the original cost.

Valuing the property at March 31, 1982

It's best to use a chartered surveyor to get a valuation, although you can estimate the value yourself. Either way, it's worth getting the Taxman to agree it before you submit your tax return. This will avoid him raising an enquiry and disputing the valuation later (which could lead to you having to pay interest and maybe even penalties). The easiest way to do this is to use the Taxman's post-transaction valuation check form, CG34, which you can download from http://www.hmrc.gov.uk/forms/cg34.pdf

Once you send the form in, the Taxman has to come back with an answer within 56 days (his published target) so he's under pressure to make a quick decision.

Tɪᴘ. Don't be conservative, go in with a valuation on the high side first. If it's agreed, then great! The higher the market value, the lower your gain. However, if it is knocked down a little, you still haven't really lost out.

4.4. TAPER RELIEF

This replaced indexation relief and applies to all property that was sold or transferred after April 5, 1998. There are two types of taper relief:

- business asset taper relief - can be claimed on the sale of certain types of commercial property and furnished holiday lettings (see 9.2. for further details of business asset taper relief)

- non-business asset taper relief - can be claimed on the sale of residential property (with the exception of furnished holiday accommodation) and any other property that doesn't qualify for business asset taper relief.

NOTE. If you owned the property before April 1998, then you can claim both indexation and taper relief.

4.4.1. Non-business asset taper relief

The relief is given as a percentage of the gain (not the purchase cost) after all other reliefs, except the annual exemption, have been claimed. The amount of relief you can claim depends on how long you have owned the property since April 5, 1998. The rates of taper relief on residential property are:

NUMBER OF COMPLETE YEARS OF OWNERSHIP SINCE APRIL 5, 1998	TAPER RELIEF (%) ON GAIN
Less than 3	Nil
3	5
4	10
5	15
6	20
7	25
8	30
9	35
10 or more	40

Use the CGT tool to calculate the taper relief for you.

Nothing in the first three years

In order to qualify for any taper relief at all, you must have held the asset for at least three complete years:

Example

Jetta purchased a property on February 1, 2002 and sold it on January 31, 2005. She didn't qualify for taper relief because she hadn't held it for three complete years. If she had sold the property on February 1, 2005, then she would have received 5% relief.

On a £100,000 gain, that's taper relief of £5,000 and a potential tax saving of £2,000 (enough to cover most solicitors' fees!)

TIP. Sell your property just after a complete year's anniversary to gain an extra year of taper relief. Make sure your solicitor (who's probably not a tax expert) is aware of this so he doesn't arrange for exchange of contracts before the crucial anniversary date.

Bonus year

If you owned the property before March 17, 1998 and sold it after April 5, 1998 then you qualify for an extra year of ownership. This is to compensate for the fact that any period of ownership before April 6, 1998 is disregarded.

Example

On April 15, 2003, Greg sells an investment property that he purchased on December 1, 1997. The qualifying period starts on April 6, 1998 and he has five complete years of ownership. This is increased to six years because he bought the property before March 17, 1998. Therefore, he can reduce his gain by 20%.

Maximum relief in ten years

In order to make sure you get the maximum 40% taper relief, you would normally need to keep your investment property for at least ten complete years.

However, if you owned the property before March 17, 1998, you can get the maximum 40% relief after only nine years.

4.4.2. Are there special rules for spouses?

Yes. Where you have transferred part or all of the property to your spouse, the period of ownership for taper relief purposes is the combined period of ownership. So, if you bought a property in June 1998, transferred it to your spouse in June 2000 and it was then sold in July 2002, your spouse could claim four years' ownership for taper relief, i.e. a 10% reduction in the gain.

4.5. CGT AVOIDANCE STRATEGY - DON'T SELL, JUST REMORTGAGE

Over the past few years, your property has risen significantly in value. Rather than sell the property (and trigger a large CGT bill), you could realise the "profit" by re-mortgaging and getting some cash out of the investment.

4.5.1. What are the short-term benefits?

If you sell a property, you will have to pay tax on any gain you make. However, if you re-mortgage the property, you have not actually made a disposal as you still own the property so there is no tax to pay on the capital you take out.

Example

Steve has an investment property in Kent which has significantly increased in value since he bought it for £40,000 in April 2003. It was recently valued at £120,000. Steve feels that the property values in Kent have levelled off, and he is now looking to invest in a new city centre development in Bristol.

In order to buy the Bristol property, Steve needs to release some of the cash tied up in his Kent property. If he sells the Kent property, he would be looking at a CGT bill of £25,120 ((£120,000 - £40,000 x 90%) - 9,200) x 40%. After repaying his original mortgage of £32,000, Steve would have £62,880 to invest in Bristol.

Instead of selling, Steve decides to re-mortgage the Kent property. The new mortgage is for 80% of the current value, £96,000. Therefore, after paying off his original mortgage, Steve has £64,000. So he now has £1,120 more to invest in Bristol than if he had sold the property.

SELL. You have made a disposal and there will be tax to pay on any gain.

RE-MORTGAGE. You have not made a disposal and still own the property so there is no tax on the capital you take out.

4.5.2. Long-term trap

CGT is based on the difference between sale proceeds and purchase cost. In order to calculate the capital gain when you sell a property, you deduct the original cost of the property and not the outstanding mortgage amount from your sale proceeds. However, where you've re-mortgaged and spent the additional funds on other properties, you could find that the "equity" left in the property is not enough to cover your CGT bill:

Example

After one year, Steve's property in Kent is proving difficult to rent so he decides to sell. As he suspected, the property value has levelled off so he sells for £120,000. The balance on the interest-only mortgage is £96,000 and he has selling costs of £4,000. With 15% taper relief, his CGT bill is therefore £22,160. Therefore, after tax, he still has to find an extra £2,160 to settle the tax bill.

TIP. Avoid getting into this situation by limiting the amount you re-mortgage by. For properties held for less than three years, the rule of thumb is to limit your borrowing to a maximum of "original cost plus 60% of any increase in value". On each anniversary up to the tenth year, you could increase your borrowing by 2% of the increase in value. After ten years, the safe haven is to make sure you don't borrow more than the "original cost plus 76% of any increase in value".

Example

If Steve had limited his borrowing using the above formula, he would have re-mortgaged to a maximum of £40,000 plus 66% of the increase. This works out as £92,800 (£40,000 + (0.66 x (£120,000 - £40,000))). By doing this, he could have paid the CGT bill and still had £1,040 left over.

Use the interactive calculator to work out the maximum amount you should re-mortgage.

NOTE. If you are using the funds to make improvements to the re-mortgaged property, then the cost of these improvements needs to be added to the original cost to work out the maximum that can be re-mortgaged.

4.6. ALLOWABLE LOSSES

You can offset any losses you make from the sale of one property against the gain on another. If you don't have any such gains, then the loss can be carried forward and set off against the first available gains in future years. If losses are carried forward, they can only be offset to the extent necessary to reduce the future gains down to the annual exemption applying for that future year.

NOTE. The loss is always offset against a gain <u>before</u> taper relief.

4.7. CGT AVOIDANCE STRATEGY - OFFSET STOCK MARKET LOSSES AGAINST YOUR PROPERTY GAIN

CGT isn't just due on gains on the sale of properties. It is also due, for example, on any gain made on the sale of shares or unit trusts. The advantage of this is that if you have made losses on shares, then you can offset this loss against any gain you make on the sale of your property.

Example

In the late 1990s, George invested £10,000 in dot.com shares, but subsequently sold them in 2006 for just £100. George also had an investment property that he sold in 2006, making a taxable gain of

£18,000. George can reduce the gain on the sale of his investment property to £8,100 by offsetting his £9,900 share loss. As George's gain is now less than his annual allowance, he ends up with no tax to pay.

4.7.1. Can I offset stock market losses from previous years?

Yes, you can. However, you need to have shown these losses on your tax return in the tax year that they occurred i.e. the year that you sold the shares.

NOTE. You only make a loss (for CGT purposes) when you actually sell the shares. Therefore, you can't normally offset any loss you've made "on paper" if you still own the shares (see 4.7.2. for the exception).

TIP. If you hadn't originally included the losses on your tax return in the year that they were made, then you can still claim the losses up to five years after the original tax return was due. So if, for example, you made losses in 2002/3, you have until January 31, 2009 to claim them. See Appendix C for a sample claim letter.

4.7.2. Do I actually have to sell the shares to claim the loss?

Usually, yes. However, the situation is different if the Taxman agrees that the quoted shares are effectively worthless (check the Taxman's negligible value list at http://www.hmrc.gov.uk/cgt/negvalist.htm).

If the shares are included on his list, then you can make a claim for the shares to be treated as though you sold them on the date you made the claim or up to two years before the tax year in which you make the claim (as long as they were worthless at the time). You can, therefore, make a loss without actually selling the shares.

TIP. You can make a negligible value claim at any time after the shares have become worthless. Therefore, defer a claim until there are sufficient gains to avoid you wasting your annual exemption (£9,200 for 2007/8).

See Appendix D for a sample negligible value claim letter.

5. Avoid CGT by using "Principal Private Residence" relief

5.1. PRINCIPAL PRIVATE RESIDENCE RELIEF

5.1.1. What is "Principal Private Residence Relief"?

You are probably aware that when you sell your own home, you don't have to pay tax on any gain you make. This is known as "Principal Private Residence" relief (PPR relief). However, as a property investor, you can use this relief to your advantage and make substantial CGT savings (often wiping out the gain completely).

5.1.2. Is it available to me?

This relief is available to you if the property has, at some time, been classed as your only or main residence.

5.1.3. How much can I claim?

This depends on whether you qualify for full or partial relief:

<u>Full relief</u>

If the property was your only or main home throughout your period of ownership (excluding the last three years, see 5.1.4.), then you can automatically claim full PPR relief so you have no CGT liability. This is regardless of the "capital gain" you make on the property.

> *Example*
>
> *Kitty buys her first home in June 1992 for £48,000. She lives in it from the date of purchase up until the day she sells it in June 2001 for £120,000. Kitty has made a capital gain of £72,000, but she pays no CGT. She can claim full residence relief because the property was her main residence throughout her period of ownership.*

<u>Partial relief</u>

If the property was your main home for only part of your period of ownership, then the amount of relief you can claim is calculated by dividing the period(s) when the property was your PPR (including the last three years of ownership (see 5.1.4) and certain other periods of absence (see 5.1.5.)) by the total length of time you owned the property.

Example

Harry buys a home in April 1993 for £50,000. He lives there until June 1995 before moving to a bigger home nearby. Harry eventually sells his original house in May 2003 for £120,000. The house was Harry's main residence for 26 months and he owned the property for a total of 121 months. Therefore, the house is treated as being Harry's PPR for 62 months (the 26 months he actually lived there plus the last 36 months) and the amount of relief he can claim is 62/121ths of £70,000. His taxable gain is £34,132.

NOTE. When calculating this relief, ignore any periods of ownership before March 31, 1982.

5.1.4. The "three year rule"

As long as the property was your main residence at some point, the last three years of ownership will also always qualify for the relief.

NOTE. If you lived in the property at any time during the last three years of ownership, you can't make a claim for the additional three years as well.

Example

Taking the first example in 5.1.3.; Kitty moves in with her partner in June 1998 and lets her original property. In this case, when she sells the property in June 2001, she can still claim maximum PPR relief. This is because the property was her main residence for six out of the nine years she owned it and, because it used to be her main residence, she is entitled to the bonus of the last three years.

TIP. Sell the property within three years of it being your main residence and avoid paying any CGT.

The "three year rule" also means you can effectively claim double PPR - on the last three years of your old property and on your new property at the same time.

5.1.5. Which other periods of absence from the property still qualify for PPR relief?

In addition to the periods when the property was actually your main residence, you can also include certain periods when you were absent from the property in order to work out the length of time it was your PPR.

NOTE. For these periods to qualify as periods of occupation, the property must actually be your main residence both before and after these absences. Also, while you're away, you can't have a different main residence.

The periods of absence that count towards PPR relief are:

- three years for any reason whatsoever (it can be a single period of three years or shorter periods as long as they don't add up to more than three years in total)
- a period of up to four years when you (or your spouse) are required to work elsewhere in the UK as part of your job
- a period of any length when you (or your spouse) are required to work abroad.

Therefore, you can have long periods of absence from the property without losing any part of your PPR exemption.

5.1.6. What happens if I've bought a property, but can't move in until it's done up?

You may not be able to move into your new property straightaway because it's still being built, needs refurbishing or you're having trouble selling your old property. However, you can still treat the new property as your PPR from the date you bought it as long as you move in within twelve months (this won't affect the PPR status of your old property because of the "three year rule"). And if you can't move in due to reasons beyond your control, you can even extend this period to two years.

5.1.7. If I move into my property after I've let it out for a few years, can I still claim PPR relief?

Yes, you can. You do not need to live in the property first in order to claim partial PPR relief for the time it was your main residence.

5.2. PRIVATE LETTING RELIEF

5.2.1. Is it available to me?

If you let out your main residence (all or part of it) as residential (not commercial) accommodation, then you can claim "Private Letting Relief". It makes no difference whether you let the property out before or after it became your main residence.

5.2.2. What's it worth?

The amount of Private Letting Relief that you can claim is the lower of:

- the amount of PPR relief
- £40,000
- the gain before letting relief is set-off (i.e. this relief cannot create a capital loss).

Therefore, if the amount of the gain covered by PPR relief is less than £40,000, then the letting relief can never be more than the PPR relief.

> *Example*
>
> *David bought a house in June 2001 for £100,000 and lived in it as his main residence for one year. He then moved out and let the property for five years before selling it in June 2007 for £250,000. David can claim PPR relief for 48 months (the twelve months he lived there plus the last three years) of the 72 months he owned the property. Therefore, £50,000 of the gain is potentially taxable. However, David can claim maximum Private Letting Relief of £40,000 (the PPR relief is £100,000), reducing his gain to just £10,000. He can also claim 20% taper relief of £2,000 and then offset the annual exemption of £9,200 so he ends up with no tax to pay. By living in the property for just one year, David has made a tax-free gain of £150,000, a tax saving of £48,000.*

5.2.3. Can a husband and wife or registered civil partners each claim the relief?

Yes! Where the property is jointly owned and jointly let by the husband and wife, each may be entitled to the £40,000 maximum relief. This makes the relief potentially very valuable.

5.3. CGT AVOIDANCE STRATEGY: "LIVE AND LET" NOT "BUY TO LET"

<u>Problem</u>

If you invest in a buy-to-let property, let it and then sell it, it will never have been your main residence. If the property has never been your home then you miss out on claiming both PPR relief and Private Letting Relief on any capital gain you make.

<u>Solution</u>

Instead of investing in a buy-to-let property, let out the house that has been your main residence and move into a new property.

<u>Tax advantage</u>

As the let property was once your main residence, the last three years of ownership are exempt from CGT (see 5.1.4.). So, if you sell the property within three years then you automatically have no tax to pay. If the property is sold after more than three years, then Private Letting Relief can reduce (or even eradicate) the capital gain.

> *Example*
>
> *Kate bought her property in 1992 for £48,000 and lived there until she moved in with her partner in June 1998. She let her original property for five years before selling it in June 2003 for £150,000. The first six years of ownership are exempt from CGT as it was her main residence. The last three years of ownership are also exempt (remember the "three year rule") because the property used to be her main residence. Ignoring indexation, that leaves a potential gain of £18,545 (2/11ths of £102,000). However, this gain is wiped out by Private Letting Relief (the gain is less than £40,000) because the property used to be Kate's main residence and was then let out. So Kate has made a tax-free gain of £102,000.*

<u>Rule of thumb</u>

You can make a CGT-free gain on your property of up to £80,000 as long as you sell the let property within 2 x (n + 3) years, where n is the number of years the property was actually your main residence.

5.4. CGT AVOIDANCE STRATEGY: "LET AND LIVE"

<u>Problem</u>

You already own an investment property that you have let out for a number of years. You have never lived in the property so will be unable to claim both PPR and Private Letting Relief. Therefore, you are facing a hefty CGT bill when you sell the property.

<u>Solution</u>

Make sure you live in the previously let property before you sell it.

<u>Tax advantage</u>

By making the property your main residence for only a short time, not only can you claim PPR relief, but you can also claim Private Letting Relief too.

> *Example*
>
> *Adam buys a property in September 2002 for £40,000 and rents it out for four years. He then lives in it for one year and sells it in September 2007 for £120,000. As the property was his main residence, the last three years are exempt (remember the "three year rule"). Therefore, the PPR relief is £48,000 (3/5ths £80,000). This leaves a gain of £32,000 which, being less than £40,000, can be completely eradicated by Private Letting Relief. By living in the property for just one year, Adam, a higher rate taxpayer, has saved £23,520 in tax (40% x ((£80,000 x 85%)- £9,200)).*

Tᴀxᴍᴀɴ Wᴀʀɴɪɴɢ! If you decide to use this strategy on a regular basis, then the Taxman will look closely to see if the property was actually your main residence.

5.4.1. Is there a minimum length of time that I have to live in the property to claim PPR relief?

The Taxman hasn't issued any specific guidance on this, but obviously, the longer you live in the property, the better chance you have of claiming PPR relief. However, the Taxman is more interested in whether the property really was your home and whether you really did live there rather than the length of time. So, the more evidence you have that it was your main residence, the more likely you are to convince him.

<u>Evidence</u>

• change your address with your local tax office. So, even his records will show that the property was your main residence!

- put utility and other bills in your own name at the property address. Typical bills include gas, electric, water, Council Tax and TV licence
- register on the voters roll at the property
- change your address with your bank, so that all statements are delivered to the property address
- hire a removal van to move enough furniture from one house to the house you want to be your main residence. Keep receipts for any new furniture delivered to the property
- don't advertise the property for sale or rent until after the period of residence
- get building work (e.g. have a new kitchen fitted) at your main home so you have to move out. Therefore, you can prove that you must be residing at the "investment" property.

5.5. CGT AVOIDANCE STRATEGY: NOMINATE A RESIDENCE

An unmarried individual or a married couple can only have one main residence for PPR relief at any one time. However, if you've got more than one home, it is possible to nominate which one you would like to be treated as your PPR. By doing this, it's possible to minimise the tax charge on both properties by switching your PPR between them.

Example

Colin, a higher rate taxpayer, owns a house in Bournemouth that he bought in 1985 for £100,000. In 2001, he also bought a house in Somerset for £150,000 which he uses mainly at the weekend. In 2007, Colin decides to sell the Somerset property for £300,000.

Without an election - the Taxman will treat his Bournemouth home as his PPR. There will be a gain of £150,000 before taper relief (20%) and the annual exemption (2007/8 £9,200). This will give rise to a CGT bill of £44,320.

With an election - when Colin bought the second property in 2001, he made an election to nominate his main residence. He elected the Bournemouth property. But in 2007, Colin made another election to switch the PPR exemption to the Somerset house. Under the "three year rule", the Somerset property is now exempt from CGT for the last three years of ownership. The gain is therefore reduced to 3/6ths £150,000, £75,000. After taper relief and the annual exemption, his CGT bill is now £20,320. Therefore, by making a simple election he has saved himself tax of £24,000.

5.5.1. How do I make the election?

The election must be made in writing to the Taxman and sent to your local tax office. See Appendix E for a sample election letter.

NOTE. In the case of a married couple, both partners must sign the election for it to be effective.

Time limit

From the date of purchasing or acquiring the second property, you have two years to tell the Taxman which one is your PPR.

TIP. You can extend the two year limit by renting a flat for a few months as a third residence. Then you can elect one of the three properties within two years of starting to rent the flat.

Changing the election

Once you've nominated a PPR, you can change it by making a similar election in writing to the Taxman. The new election can be backdated by up to two years. See Appendix F for a sample variation of election letter.

TIP. When making the election, choose the property that is most likely to make a bigger capital gain or be sold first. If you do end up selling the other one first, then you can simply change the election before you sell it.

5.5.2. What happens if I don't make an election?

If you own two or more properties, and haven't told the Taxman which one is your main residence within the two-year time limit, he will make the decision for you based on, for example, the time spent in each property, or which is the main postal address.

It is possible that the Taxman might question whether the second property ever became a PPR so you will need evidence of occupation. As well as considering the factors in 5.4.1., it's worth keeping a diary showing the dates of overnight stays.

TIP. Make the election to nominate your PPR as soon as you acquire the second property. That way, you can make another election at any time in the future to switch your PPR.

5.5.3. How long does the nominated property have to be my PPR to qualify for relief?

As long as it qualifies as a residence, it doesn't matter how short you elect it as your PPR - as little as a week would be acceptable.

Encouragingly the Taxman includes such an example in his CGT manual at CG64512 (http://www.hmrc.gov.uk/manuals/cg4manual/CG64512.htm).

5.6. SELLING LAND THAT IS PART OF YOUR MAIN RESIDENCE

A property developer may be interested in buying part of your home's garden in order to build new houses. So, if you decide to sell the land, do you have to pay CGT?

Half a hectare

If the total area of the garden is less than half a hectare (just over an acre), then the Taxman will readily accept the land as being part of your main residence. Therefore, you will be able to claim full PPR relief and any gain will be exempt from CGT.

If the property was your home and has subsequently been let as private residential accommodation, then you can still claim partial PPR relief and Private Letting Relief where the garden is less than half a hectare.

5.6.1. What happens if my garden is more than half a hectare?

If you've got more than half a hectare of grounds, you should argue an increase in the area that's classed as garden so that a larger area can be CGT-exempt. A number of taxpayers have tried to extend the half a hectare limit to reflect the size and character of their homes. The argument being that a larger area is required for the reasonable enjoyment of a larger house. Some have been successful, some not. If you manage to increase the exempt area, you also reduce the taxable area. If you think a bigger area is appropriate, then try and negotiate this with the Taxman in advance.

5.6.2. Would it be better to sell the property before I sell the land?

No. Case law has decided that if you sell your main residence before you sell the land, then you are unable to claim PPR relief on the sale of the land. This is because the land is no longer attached to your main residence. So, if you were thinking of moving or now don't fancy living next to a building site, be very careful what you sell first.

TIP. So you don't lose your PPR exemption:

- sell the land wanted for building before you sell the house and remaining garden
- do not let development work take place before the land is sold
- do not fence off the development plot until it is sold.

5.6.3. CGT avoidance strategy: develop and move

Problem

Rather than just sell off part of your garden, you want to maximise profits by developing it first (i.e. building a new house in the grounds) and then selling it off. However, this will mean that the developed land is no longer part of your main residence and therefore much of your profit could be swallowed up by a hefty tax bill.

Solution

Move into the newly built property and sell your old house. Your old property will qualify for full PPR relief as long as it's sold within three years (the "three year rule" 5.1.4.). You will also be entitled to PPR relief on your new house as long as you move in within twelve months of the development starting (5.1.6.).

5.7. MAKING USE OF YOUR CHILDREN

Every unmarried individual can have a main residence and this includes your children. And, if they have a main residence, they will be entitled to claim PPR relief when they sell the property.

If you have children going away to college or university, then you may want to buy them a house nearby as both an investment for their future and somewhere semi-decent for them to live. If you decide to do this, make sure that it is structured correctly to make maximum use of various reliefs.

The property should be purchased in your child's name. There shouldn't be a problem getting finance for this as long as you are prepared to put down the deposit and act as guarantor on the mortgage. The rental income received from letting spare rooms to other students should be sufficient to cover the mortgage repayments. Your child will also be able to claim "rent-a-room" relief on the rental income so there will be no tax for them to pay on the first £4,250 of rental profits (see 1.4.).

As long as the property is your child's only property, it will be regarded as their main residence and PPR relief will be available on the sale of it.

NOTE. The Taxman will generally accept that taking in lodgers does not restrict the availability of PPR. A "lodger" is someone who, whilst having their own bedroom, will otherwise live as part of the owner's household. Student friends would, therefore, qualify as lodgers.

5.7.1. Can I receive any of the proceeds once my child has sold the property?

As long as you give the mortgage deposit to your child with no strings attached and they are not contractually obligated to give you a share of the proceeds, then there is no reason why they can't make a generous gift to you once they have sold the property!

6. The tax implications of gifting properties

6.1. AVOIDING CGT WHEN TRANSFERRING PROPERTY TO SOMEONE OTHER THAN YOUR SPOUSE

Spouses can freely transfer ownership of properties between each other without having to pay Capital Gains Tax (CGT). Unfortunately, the same exemption does not apply to unmarried or unregistered couples. However, with some careful planning, you can still transfer properties to an unmarried partner, your children, or anyone else for that matter, tax-free.

6.1.1. Make use of the annual exemption and transfer in stages

If you want to transfer a residential investment property (i.e. it's not your Principal Private Residence) to someone other than a spouse, then consider doing it in stages over a number of years. You can then take advantage of your annual CGT allowance to wipe out your CGT bill.

Example

Sue and Paul bought an investment property for £55,000 in June 2003 with the intention of giving it to their two daughters Valerie and Lucy in 2007/8 when they are both over 18. However, in 2007/8, the property is worth £105,000. So, if they transfer the property to their daughters now, they are facing a £20,000 CGT bill as higher rate taxpayers.

Therefore, they decide to transfer £9,200 (8.8%) of the property to each of their daughters in 2007/8 in order to make use of each of their annual CGT allowances but without triggering a CGT bill. In 2008/9, they will make another transfer of the property to their daughters equal to that year's annual allowance. They will continue doing this until they have transferred the entire property tax-free.

NOTE. The part transfer of property can be tricky so make sure you get yourself a good solicitor and weigh up the legal costs versus the savings.

6.1.2. Transfer in a low income year

If your income is likely to be lower in a future tax year, then wait to transfer the property. If your income is below the higher rate band (i.e. less than £34,600 for 2007/8), you can potentially halve your CGT liability by paying the lower 20% rate instead of 40%.

6.2. HOW TO AVOID CGT ON GIFTS OF HOLIDAY HOMES

The normal rules for residential investment properties are that if you give your property away to anyone other than your spouse, then you have to pay CGT based on the market value of the property at the date of the gift. However, if you've got a property that qualifies as a furnished holiday home (see 3.2. for qualifying criteria), then you may be able to take advantage of the very generous "gift (also known as "holdover") relief". By claiming this relief, you can avoid paying CGT when you give a property to, for example, an unmarried partner or your children.

6.2.1. What is "gift relief"?

When you dispose of a qualifying holiday home, you can ask for the capital gain to be "held over". In other words, the capital gain is passed on to the person you give the property to. This is achieved by them being treated as purchasing the property at its original cost to you (plus indexation allowance, if applicable). Therefore, when they eventually sell the property, they will pay tax on any increase in value from the date you purchased the property and not from the date you gave it to them.

6.2.2. How do I make a claim?

You can make a claim by using the form on the back of the Taxman's help sheet IR295 available from http://www.hmrc.gov.uk/helpsheets/ir295.pdf. This form needs to be signed by both you and the person you give the property to.

You don't have to include a calculation of the gain with your claim as long as you complete the second page of the form.

6.2.3. Is there a time limit for making the claim?

You need to make a claim within five years and ten months of the end of the tax year in which you make the gift. So, if you make a gift in July 2007, you have until January 31, 2014 to make the claim.

6.2.4. So how will it work if I want to give a holiday home to one of my children?

You have a furnished holiday home that you would like to give to one of your children without paying CGT. When you give them the property, you both need to sign a "gift relief election" (see 6.2.2.). This will mean that your child is deemed to have acquired the property at a price equal to what you paid for it. You are deemed to have sold the holiday home at that price. So, there's no CGT for you to pay because your sale price equals your purchase price.

6.2.5. But doesn't this mean that my child will pay more CGT when they eventually sell the property?

Not necessarily. If your child lives in the property and makes it their main residence (see 5.4.1. for guidance on how to do this), there could be no CGT to pay when they sell the property.

There will be no CGT to pay as long as the property was your child's main residence throughout their period of ownership. In this case, the total gain that they would have paid tax on is exempt. And, due to the gift relief election, this total gain will include any gain arising during your period of ownership.

6.2.6. Can I receive any of the proceeds once my child has sold the property?

This would be the ultimate tax avoidance; selling the property via your child and converting a large taxable gain into a tax-free one. Therefore, it's likely to be looked at very closely by the Taxman. However, as long as you make the gift to your child absolute i.e. with no strings attached, it would be difficult for him to make a successful challenge. Of course, this doesn't prevent your child from making a generous gift to you some time in the future!

6.2.7. CGT avoidance strategy - don't gift the holiday home, sell it at undervalue

The problem with giving a property away is that you won't receive any proceeds (unless your offspring are generous enough to give you part of the proceeds later!). So, rather than give the property away, you could sell it at undervalue. However, where you sell at undervalue, the gain that is held over is reduced by the excess of the sale proceeds over the cost. By selling at the right price and signing a gift relief exemption, you could still avoid CGT altogether.

The right price

Sell the property for a price equal to the total of:

- your original purchase price
- the costs of improvements
- the annual exemption.

By doing this, you'll have no tax to pay as you can elect to holdover the whole gain. The proceeds do not exceed the cost.

You could also take taper relief into account when working out the maximum proceeds. If you are the sole owner of a furnished holiday home which you've owned for more than two years, then you're entitled to 75% taper relief (see 9.2.). For 2007/8, this means you can have a gain of up to £9,200/0.25 plus the cost and still pay no CGT.

> *Example*
>
> *Mary and Anthony jointly own a holiday cottage in the Cotswolds which qualifies as a furnished holiday home. They have now decided to sell the home to their daughter, Olivia, at a price that will mean they pay no CGT. They originally purchased the cottage in 2000 for £80,000 and it is now worth £250,000. They can make a claim to holdover the gain and avoid CGT if they sell the property for less than the cost of £80,000 plus their annual exemptions (2 x £9,200). The gain that's held-over will be £151,600 and the allowable cost to Olivia will be £98,400 i.e. what she paid. By holding-over the gain Mary and Anthony will save £9,640 in tax. If Olivia then lives in the property as her main residence, she can sell the cottage tax-free.*
>
> *If Mary and Anthony also took taper relief into account, they could actually receive proceeds of £153,600 without paying any CGT. This is because they've owned the property for over two years and are therefore able to claim the maximum 75% business asset taper relief. The gain before taper relief would be £73,600 (£153,600 - £80,000). After 75% taper relief, the gain would be £18,400 (£9,200 each) which is covered by their annual exemptions. The gain held over would be £96,400 and the cost to Olivia will again be what she's paid i.e. £153,600.*

6.3. USING TRUSTS TO AVOID CGT

Usually, you can only claim gift relief (6.2.1.) when you transfer furnished holiday accommodation or certain types of commercial property to someone else. However, you can avoid paying CGT on any type of property by transferring it into certain types of trust.

6.3.1. What is a trust?

A trust is formed when one person (the settlor) gives some assets to somebody else (the trustee) to use for the benefit of others (the beneficiaries). There are two main types of trust, discretionary and non-discretionary.

Up to 21 March, 2006, gift relief was only available for transfers into discretionary trusts. From 22 March, 2006, gift relief is also available for transfers into most interest in possession and accumulation and maintenance trusts created on or after that date.

6.3.2. What is a discretionary trust?

As its name suggests, in a discretionary trust, the trustees have discretion in deciding when and to whom (of the beneficiaries) payments of trust income or capital are made. No beneficiary has the right to demand income from a discretionary trust.

6.3.3. Does the trust have to pay tax on its income and gains?

Yes. The trust is subject to income tax and CGT in the same way as individuals. Both are taxed at 40%. Trusts have an annual CGT exemption which is half that of an individual (i.e. £4,600 for 2007/8).

The trustees have to complete a tax return in exactly the same way as individuals. The filing deadlines and tax payment dates are also the same.

A discretionary trust may also have to pay Inheritance Tax (IHT) if its value is more than the IHT nil-rate band (£300,000 for 2007/8). On every tenth anniversary there will be a charge of no more than 6% of the trust value and, at eventual exit, a further maximum 6% charge.

6.3.4. How do I set up a discretionary trust?

Anyone over 18 can set up a trust in the UK to hold UK property. A solicitor should be able to set one up (by drafting a trust deed) for you for around £250 to £500 plus VAT.

6.3.5. How do I put the property into a discretionary trust?

You can transfer the property into a trust as a gift. As with gifts to other people, the property is treated as being transferred at its market value.

However, you can elect to have this gain held-over (see 6.2.1.), which means that you won't pay any CGT.

NOTE. Any transfer into a discretionary trust is a chargeable transfer for IHT purposes (see 6.5.). This means that if you transfer a property into a discretionary trust, you may have to pay IHT of 20%. However, provided the value of the property is less than the nil-rate band (£300,000 for 2007/8), you will avoid paying tax on the transfer.

6.4. TAX AVOIDANCE STRATEGY - USING TRUSTS TO DEFER CGT ON RESIDENTIAL PROPERTY GIFTS

Problem

If you have an investment property that you have never lived in, it's likely that you will pay CGT on any gain you make when you transfer it.

Solution

As long as the property is worth less than £300,000, you can transfer it into a discretionary trust without paying any CGT or IHT. As the settlor, you would elect for any gain from the gift into the trust to be held-over.

Therefore, you have deferred the CGT liability, but the gain will still be chargeable on any subsequent disposal by the beneficiary (or beneficiaries).

NOTE. If you gift a property to a trust in which you have some sort of interest, then, since December 10, 2003, you cannot claim gift relief.

6.4.1. Can the trust beneficiaries live in the property and claim PPR relief?

No. Before December 2003, there was a specific tax avoidance scheme where a discretionary trust was used to defer a gain on a property that is then occupied by one of the beneficiaries as their main residence. On disposal of the property by the trustees the whole gain is exempt from CGT under the main residence exemption rules. However, since December 2003, either the gain on transfer to the trust can be deferred or PPR relief can subsequently be claimed, but not both.

6.5. INHERITANCE TAX ON LIFETIME GIFTS

As you are probably aware, you may have to pay Inheritance Tax (IHT) on the value of your estate (basically everything you own - all your assets minus anything you owe) when you die. You also have to pay IHT on certain gifts you make while you are alive. These are known as "chargeable lifetime transfers" and occur when you gift an asset into a discretionary trust (see 6.3.2.).

Also, if you decide to gift a property to someone else without putting it into a discretionary trust, then the person you are gifting the property to could incur IHT on the gift if you die within seven years of making the gift. These are known as "potentially exempt transfers" (PETs).

Therefore, before you decide to gift properties, it is important to understand the potential IHT implications.

6.5.1. What are the basic principles of IHT?

IHT is a tax charged on the value of your property and other assets in your estate at the date of death, less any outstanding loans. IHT on death is charged at the following rates:

- on the first £300,000 (2007/8) - 0%.
- on the balance of the estate over £300,000 (2007/8) - 40%.

The first £300,000 of your estate is known as the "nil-rate band".

IHT on "chargeable lifetime transfers" i.e. gifts into discretionary and some other trusts, is charged at 20% if over the "nil-rate band".

<u>Exempt gifts</u>

Certain gifts are exempt from IHT altogether. These include:

- gifts between UK domiciled spouses (if your spouse is not domiciled in the UK, then the exemption is restricted to £55,000)
- gifts to charities.

<u>Seven-year rule</u>

Any gifts you make, apart from transfers into chargeable trusts, are IHT-free as long as you manage to survive seven years after making the gift (a PET). If you die within seven years, the recipients will have to pay IHT, but on a sliding scale. If you die within three years, they have to pay 40% of anything above the nil-rate band. If, however, you die after three years, the tax reduces by 20% for each additional year survived.

6.5.2. Can I give a property away, but continue to live in it?

No, the property must be given outright. For instance, if you give your house to your children, but carry on living in it without paying the full market rent, that would be a gift with "reservation of benefit". This would still be counted as part of your estate when you die even if you live more than seven years.

Market rent

If you do want to continue living in a property, then you need to make sure that you pay a market rent for the privilege. A local firm of surveyors would be able to provide a rent value.

6.5.3. How does IHT interact with CGT?

As long as you give away your properties more than seven years before you die then you will avoid IHT. However, gifting property during your lifetime will result in a CGT charge on any gains. You can avoid CGT by not gifting properties during your lifetime, but then your estate will suffer IHT on any amounts over £300,000 (2007/8). So, you always need to consider both IHT and CGT in deciding whether to transfer properties to someone other than your spouse.

6.6. IHT (AND CGT) AVOIDANCE STRATEGY: EQUITY RELEASE

In 4.5, we looked at a CGT avoidance strategy where you can withdraw funds from your investment properties by re-mortgaging the properties rather than selling them. This can also be a very effective way of limiting the amount of IHT you have to pay.

Problem

You've built up a decent portfolio of investment properties and you now want to pass this on to your children. However, if you just gift them the properties, you will have to pay CGT on any gains you've made. So, how can you transfer the properties to your children, avoiding CGT and IHT in the process?

Solution

For IHT purposes, the value of your properties included in your estate is their market value less any outstanding loans. So, you mortgage up to the hilt on your properties, and then gift the cash raised to the children. Cash is not a capital asset, so there's no CGT to pay on the transfer.

Provided you survive seven years from the date of the transfer, there will also be no IHT to pay on it. Therefore, you have reduced the value of your estate and IHT will only be payable on the net value of the properties (you've re-mortgaged so the high level of borrowings will keep the IHT bill down).

When should I re-mortgage?

Deciding when to re-mortgage your properties and give away the cash is a difficult balancing act. Ideally, you have to pitch it so that you're young enough to have the maximum chance of surviving seven years, but not so young that it is difficult to decide how much you can afford to give away without depriving yourself of a decent lifestyle. While your children may very well be willing to hand back any money you need later on, they may not be able to do so. They may, for instance, have lost it in a divorce settlement or simply frittered it away.

Tip. You can take out insurance to pay the IHT should you die within seven years. The amount of the premium depends on your age and health, but could save your children (or other recipients) substantial amounts of IHT.

6.7. TAX AVOIDANCE STRATEGY: SPOUSES SET UP DISCRETIONARY WILL TRUSTS

Problem

You and your spouse own several properties with relatively small mortgages. The value of each of your shares in these properties is over the IHT threshold. If you and your spouse make wills leaving all your respective estates to each other and providing that, after the death of the surviving spouse, the combined estates pass to your children, then no tax will be payable on the first death (because gifts to spouses are exempt - see 6.5.1.). On the second death, tax will be payable on the aggregate of the two estates:

- at 0% on the first £300,000 (the 2007/8 nil rate band) and
- at 40% on the balance.

> *Example*
>
> *Ozzie and Harriet make wills leaving their respective estates to each other and then to their children on the death of the survivor. Ozzie has assets worth £300,000 and Harriet also has assets worth £300,000. Ozzie dies before Harriet.*
>
> *On Ozzie's death, his £300,000 estate passes to Harriet and there is no IHT to pay as transfers to spouses are exempt from IHT.*

On Harriet's death, her estate is now worth £600,000 (her estate of £300,000 plus £300,000 inherited from Ozzie). Therefore, the IHT payable will be £120,000 (40% (£600,000 - £300,000)).

Ozzie might be said to be "wasting" his nil-rate band. The whole of his estate is exempt because he is giving it all to his wife, but he could give as much as £300,000 to his children and the rest to his wife without any tax being payable. If, instead of Ozzie leaving all his estate to Harriet, he had left a legacy of £300,000 to his children and the residue to his wife, he would have been able to make use of his own nil-rate band.

In this case, Ozzie and Harriet make wills leaving legacies of £300,000 to their children and the residue to each other. On Ozzie's death, there won't be any IHT to pay. And on Harriet's death, there still won't be any IHT to pay.

An overall tax saving of £120,000!

However, the disadvantage of you giving £300,000 to your children and the balance of your estate to your spouse is that it may result in your spouse facing financial hardship, if the balance left to them is inadequate to support their needs.

Solution

The use of a discretionary trust solves this problem. Instead of giving £300,000 directly to the children, it is transferred to a discretionary trust for the benefit of:

- your surviving spouse
- your children
- any other individual you care to name.

NOTE. If you jointly own some of the properties, you need to make sure they are owned as "tenants-in-common" (see 7.2.1.) and not joint tenants. Only as tenants-in-common can your half interest in a property be transferred into a discretionary trust.

By including your surviving spouse as a beneficiary, you still save the £120,000 in tax and yet, if necessary, the trustees can pay out income or underlying capital to the surviving spouse at their discretion (often with regard to your "letter of wishes").

Letter of wishes

If you are setting up a discretionary will trust, then you will normally write a separate letter of wishes. These letters are not legally binding and the trustees do not have to follow your wishes (as this would make the trust non-discretionary). The letter will usually state that the first aim of the trust is to ensure that adequate provision is made for the surviving spouse for the remainder of their days. The letter will usually say what is desired to happen thereafter, such as passing property to your children.

See Appendix G for a sample Letter of Wishes.

WARNING! This strategy assumes that your nil-rate band will be used up with your investment properties. Where all or part of the nil-rate band will need to be satisfied by a transfer of the family home, additional structuring will be required. This is because the Taxman may argue that your surviving spouse has an "interest in possession" in the house by virtue of their full-time occupation of the property as a beneficiary of the trust. This would defeat the use of the trust, as retaining an interest in possession means that the value of the property falls into the surviving spouse's estate.

6.7.1. How much does it cost to set up a discretionary will trust?

A discretionary will trust is much more complicated and difficult to understand than a simple will under which you give everything to your spouse, or if they are not living, to your children. You should expect to pay at least £300 + VAT for each will.

Section III

Buying strategies to avoid tax

7. Buying a property in joint names

Many people buy their first investment property in their sole name. However, buying a property jointly can have significant tax savings. This chapter looks at the tax effects of owning a property jointly, firstly with your with your spouse, and then with someone else.

7.1. JOINT OWNERSHIP WITH YOUR SPOUSE

Owning property in joint names with your spouse can lead to both income tax and Capital Gains Tax (CGT) savings. This is particularly true where one of you is a higher rate taxpayer and the other has little, or no, income.

7.1.1. Can I save income tax on my rental profits if I transfer the property to my spouse?

Sole owner

If you are the sole owner of a property and let it out, you have to pay tax on any profit (rent less expenses) you make (see 1.2.). The rate of income tax depends on your total income during the tax year. For 2007/8, if your other income is more than £39,825 then you will be paying tax at the higher rate of 40%.

> *Example 1*
>
> *Peter is a director of a company and receives a salary of £60,000. He also has an investment property which he rents out for £500 a month (£6,000 a year). His rental expenses for the year were £2,000. Therefore, Peter has to pay tax of £1,600 on his rental income ((£6,000 - £2,000) x 40%).*

Transfer to spouse

If one of you is a higher rate taxpayer whilst the other is not paying any tax at all (or paying tax at the basic rate), then you can make significant income tax savings by transferring the investment property either into joint names or into the sole name of the spouse with the lower income. Your spouse will not be taxed at the higher rate on their rental income until their total income for the year exceeds £39,825 (2007/8).

> *Example 2*
>
> *Peter's wife, Sam, doesn't work and has no other income. Peter decides to transfer the property into her name. As Sam has no other income, the whole £4,000 rental profit is covered by her tax-free personal allowance (£5,225 for 2007/8). As there is no tax to pay on the rental profits, they save £1,600.*
>
> *If Sam has a job and earns £20,000 a year, it would still be beneficial for Peter to transfer the property into her name. In this case, she would pay 22% tax on the rental profits of £880, still a saving of £720.*

Joint ownership

There may be situations where it is preferable for you to each have a share in the property. For example, you may both be basic rate taxpayers with similar income. However, if you were the sole owner of the property, the rental income would take you into the higher rate band. By owning the property jointly, you both have a share of the rental income and stay below the higher rate band.

> *Example 3*
>
> *Peter has a salary of £39,000 a year and Sam's is £25,000. The rental income from the investment property is £4,000 a year. If Peter were the sole owner of the property, he would pay 22% tax on the first £825 of rental income (taking his total income for the year up to the £39,825 threshold), but would pay 40% tax on the remainder. Therefore, the tax on his rental income would be £1,451.*
>
> *If Peter and Sam jointly own the property, then the rental income will be split between them. In this case, all of Sam's share will be taxed at 22% and the first £825 of Peter's will be. Assuming the rental income is split equally, owning the property jointly has saved them £360 a year.*

NOTE. If you are both higher rate taxpayers, there are no income tax advantages to buying the property with your spouse. However, there could still be significant CGT savings (see 7.1.4.).

7.1.2. If I own a property jointly with my spouse, do we always have to split the rental profits equally?

There are situations where it may be preferable to split the income in unequal proportions.

Example

Taking Example 3 above, it would be preferable for Sam to have a greater share of the rental profits so that she can avoid paying any higher rate tax. If Peter received 20% (£800) of the profits with Sam receiving 80% (£3,200), then neither of them would pay tax at the higher rate and their total tax bill would be £880. A saving of £211 compared with sharing the profits equally.

The problem is that where you hold a property jointly with your spouse, the Taxman automatically treats you and your spouse as sharing the income 50:50. This is the case even if you don't actually own the investment in equal shares.

However, if you don't own the property in equal proportions, you can jointly elect to be taxed on your actual shares. To do this you must both complete and sign a "declaration" form (Form 17 which you can download from http://www.hmrc.gov.uk/forms/form17.pdf) and send it to the Taxman.

Evidence

You have to give the Taxman proof of anything other than a 50:50 split. This means that if you want a 75:25 split of the rental profits, you need to show that the property is owned 75:25.

However, it seems that different tax offices are asking for different information. Some will accept a signed declaration by both parties that ownership of the joint asset is no longer 50:50 but now some other proportion. Other tax offices want copies of more formal property documents, such as "declaration of trust" (see 7.2.5.). Our advice is to send in just a signed declaration, but be ready to provide further information if requested.

7.1.3. Tax avoidance strategy: Split the income but retain ownership

Problem

As mentioned in 7.1.1., transferring the property either partly or wholly to your lower income spouse can lead to considerable income tax savings. However, this tax planning is only effective when the beneficial title in the property is genuinely transferred to your spouse. The problem is that you may not want to give your spouse a large share in the property. So, how can you save income tax on your rental profits without giving up too much of your ownership of the property?

Solution

If you solely own a property, follow these steps to retain majority ownership, and pay less income tax - the best of both worlds!

1. Transfer the property into joint ownership (see 7.2. and seek advice from your solicitor)

2. Transfer only 1% beneficial ownership to your spouse, so that you retain 99% ownership

3. Don't elect for the income to be split by the beneficial ownership percentages

Under the 50:50 rule, tax law automatically treats you as sharing the income equally even if you don't actually own the investment in equal shares.

7.1.4. Can I save CGT if I own the property jointly with my spouse?

By owning a property with your spouse, you can also make substantial tax savings when you come to sell the property. This is because each individual has an annual CGT allowance, currently £9,200 for 2007/8 (see 4.1.5.). Therefore, you and your spouse can each use the exemption to reduce your part of the gain. So, when you sell the property, the first £18,400 of the gain (assuming no other gains in the year) will be tax-free.

> *Example*
>
> *Adam solely owns an investment property which has made a capital gain of £50,000 when he comes to sell it in September 2007. As a higher rate taxpayer, he will pay tax of £16,320 (40% x (£50,000 - £9,200)).*
>
> *However, if Adam and his wife, Natalie (both higher rate taxpayers), jointly own the property, then they each have an annual exemption to offset against the gain. Therefore, the maximum tax on the gain will be £12,640 (40% x (£50,000 - £18,400)). A saving of £3,680.*

The situation is even better if your spouse doesn't have any other income. In this case, they will pay CGT at only 10% for the first £2,230 over the annual exempt amount and 20% on the remainder of their share of the capital gain up to £34,600 for 2007/8.

> *Example*
>
> *Adam and Natalie jointly own the property, but in this case, Natalie doesn't work and has no other income. The tax they will pay on the £50,000 gain will be £9,257 - a saving of £7,063 compared with Adam owning the property solely in his own name.*

7.1.5. If I own a property jointly with my spouse, will the capital gains automatically be split 50:50?

No. The capital gain will be split according to the proportion of ownership. So, if you own 75% of the property, you will be allocated 75% of the gain.

Tip. If your spouse pays tax at a lower rate than you, transfer a greater proportion of the property to them. This way, a larger part of the gain will be taxed at the lower rate.

As a rule of thumb, you should try to make sure that the higher rate taxpayer's share of the gain is no more than twice the annual allowance (i.e. £18,400 for 2007/8). Above this figure, the benefits of the annual CGT allowance are outweighed by the additional higher rate tax paid.

7.1.6. Can I transfer half the property to my spouse before I sell it to make use of their annual exemption?

Yes, you can. Spouses can transfer ownership of properties between each other without incurring CGT (see 4.1.4.). Just make sure that you have a non-tax avoidance reason for doing so (e.g. it was a birthday present) and that the transfer is made before putting the property on the market.

7.2. HOW DO I TRANSFER PART OF A PROPERTY TO MY SPOUSE?

If you decide to transfer a property to your spouse (or anyone else for that matter), then you will need to let your solicitor know what type of joint ownership you want.

7.2.1. What are the different types of joint ownership?

Note. The legal terms used to describe the different types of ownership make reference to "tenants". This makes it seem as though it's about rented property. This is not the case - it's just legal jargon!

If you decide to own a house jointly with someone else (whether it's your spouse, partner, relative or friend), you can own it in one of two ways - as joint tenants or tenants-in-common.

Joint tenants

Here, the joint owners do not have particular shares in the property; they own the whole thing together. When one owner dies, the property automatically becomes the possession of the other owner(s). Because no joint owner has a defined share, their interest in the property does not become part of their estate when they die, but simply disappears. This means that a will made by the first joint tenant to die, which leaves the property to someone else, would be ineffective.

A husband and wife are normally treated as owning joint property as joint tenants so they have equal rights over the property and when one dies, the other automatically owns all of it.

If you own a property as joint tenants then your rental profits and capital gains will be divided equally between you.

Tenants-in-common

Each owner has a defined share of the property. They can decide between themselves what proportion of the property belongs to each owner. When the property is sold, each owner is entitled to his or her percentage share of the sale proceeds. If one of the owners dies, their share is added to their estate and does not automatically pass to the other tenants-in-common.

Note. If you don't specify that you want different shares then the law assumes that the shares are equal i.e. if there are two owners, this will automatically be half each, if three owners, a third each and so on.

It's only if you and your spouse own a property in unequal shares as tenants-in-common, that you can elect to have your rental profits split in the proportions of your ownership (see 7.1.2.). Any capital gain will automatically be divided between you according to your proportion of ownership (see 7.1.5.).

7.2.2. Which method should I use?

Joint tenants

This is most suitable for you and your spouse where the combined value of your properties is likely to be under the Inheritance Tax threshold (i.e. under £300,000 for 2007/8). If you have a main residence and a separate buy-to-let investment property, this is unlikely to be the case.

Tenants-in-common

This is more suitable form of ownership when:

* you are not married to the other owners (e.g. family, friends, business associates, unmarried partners) or

* the combined value of you and your spouse's property is over the Inheritance Tax threshold (i.e. over £300,000 for 2007/8) or

- you need to have unequal shares in a property, for example to save income tax (7.1.2.) or CGT (7.1.5.).

Note. You may be able to change from joint tenants to tenants-in-common at a later date, but you will not be able to change back from tenants-in-common to joint tenants.

7.2.3. How do I change from joint tenants to tenants-in-common?

If you currently own the property as joint tenants then it is relatively simple to change to tenants-in-common. However, we would recommend that you seek advice from a solicitor before doing this.

Warning! Consider the consequences of severing a joint tenancy carefully. If you are actually living in the property and choose to sever the joint tenancy, the death of your partner could mean that you are prematurely forced to sell the house. You will not automatically receive your partner's share in the property should he or she die, as would have been the case had the joint tenancy been preserved. This can, of course, be overcome by making sure that your partner's share of the property is left to you in their will, but you may not want to do this for Inheritance Tax reasons.

Notice of severance

To change from joint tenants to tenants-in-common, all you need to do is to give the other person a formal notice of severance (they don't have to agree). This must be in writing, and all that is necessary to say is:

> "I *(insert name)* give notice to *(insert names of other co-owners)* of my intention to sever the joint tenancy of *(insert address)*. Dated *(insert date)*" and make sure you sign it!

Send it by recorded or registered post.

Changing shares

Unless the severance notice says otherwise, the joint tenancy will become a tenancy-in-common in equal shares. You can change the actual proportion of ownership by asking your solicitor to draw up a separate declaration of trust.

7.2.4. What should be included in a declaration of trust?

If the way in which you choose to own your property is as tenants-in-common then you should have a declaration of trust. This records the arrangement between the joint owners. The trust deed should state:

- the percentage share that each owner has, i.e. you might say that one person has a 25% share and the other has a 75% share and that if the property were sold then the money would be divided in that way

- if there is a mortgage on the property, then the trust deed should provide for this to be paid off before dividing the sale proceeds. The trust deed should also define the proportions in which the two owners would make the mortgage payments.

7.2.5. Should I transfer part of the mortgage debt to my spouse?

If you transfer part of the property to your spouse and they also take over responsibility for part of the mortgage, then that proportion is treated as sale proceeds and Stamp Duty Land Tax (see 10.2.) will be due on the transfer unless the debt transferred is less than £125,000.

Tip. When you transfer a proportion of the property to your spouse, make sure you don't transfer the mortgage. This way you will avoid Stamp Duty Land Tax on the transfer.

7.3. JOINT OWNERSHIP WITH SOMEONE OTHER THAN YOUR SPOUSE

7.3.1. Can I save income tax if I transfer the property to someone other than my spouse?

Yes, you can. However, the problem is that you can't usually transfer a property to a non-spouse without incurring a potential CGT bill (see 4.1.3.). Therefore, it would be better to buy a property in joint names from the outset, rather than transfer it at a later date.

Once the property is in joint names, the income tax savings are the same as for joint ownership between spouses (see 7.1.1.). Again, you will make the largest income tax savings where you are a higher rate taxpayer and your co-owner (or owners) pays no tax or tax at the basic rate.

7.3.2. How is the income split if I own a property with someone other than my spouse?

As mentioned in 7.1.2, all property jointly owned between spouses is treated as an equal 50:50 split unless they make an election otherwise. However, this is not the case for property owned between non-spouses. In this situation, the split of income is based on the proportion of ownership in the property.

7.3.3. Can I save CGT if I own a property with someone other than my spouse?

Yes. The CGT savings on sale of a property are exactly the same as for spouses (see 7.1.4.). Again, any gain will be split according to the proportion of ownership.

7.3.4. Can I transfer half the property to someone before I sell it to make use of their annual exemption?

As mentioned in 7.3.1., where you transfer a property to someone other than your spouse, the market value of the property at the time of the transfer must be used to work out any taxable gain. However, by transferring a property into joint names with someone other than your spouse prior to sale could still save you CGT.

> *Example*
>
> *Jack bought an investment property several years ago and has now decided to sell. After various reliefs (except the annual allowance), he estimates that the capital gain will be £120,000. His other income makes him a higher rate taxpayer, so he would be facing a CGT bill of £44,320 (assuming the 2007/8 CGT allowance of £9,200) when he sells the property.*
>
> *Therefore, Jack decides to transfer half the property to his son, Matthew, in the 2007/8 tax year. When he makes the transfer, he will have to pay CGT on the market value of the amount transferred (i.e. half of the total value of the property). He will, therefore, have a CGT bill of £20,320 when he makes the transfer.*
>
> *In 2008/9, both Jack and Matthew decide to jointly sell the property. The property hasn't increased much in value since last year so Matthew will pay no CGT on his share of the gain. Assuming the annual exemption stayed the same, Jack would have another CGT bill for £20,320. Therefore, Jack has made an overall tax saving of £3,680 (40% of the annual exemption).*

NOTE. Transferring a property to someone else has possible Inheritance Tax implications (see 6.5.). And as in 7.1.6. make sure you have a non-tax avoidance reason for making the transfer or the Taxman might try to challenge the arrangement.

7.3.5. Can I own a property jointly with more than one person?

Yes, you can. In this case, the potential tax savings could be even greater as any gain on the eventual sale would be divided between the different partners with each partner being able to use their annual CGT allowance. Selling a property jointly owned by you and three other people could save you up to £11,040 in CGT in 2007/8 ((£9,200 x 3) x 40%).

You can only register a maximum of four legal owners of a property with the Land Registry (or show four legal owners on the title deeds if the property isn't registered).

However, you could have more than four tenants-in-common (i.e. more than four beneficial owners), each entitled to a proportion of the proceeds when the property is sold (as detailed in a declaration of trust - see 7.2.4.).

7.3.6. Does a mortgage on the property have to be in the names of all the owners?

A lender will require the mortgage to be a charge over the legal title of the property. If the legal title is in joint names, then the mortgage will also have to be in joint names.

However, as it is possible for someone to be a beneficial owner without being a legal owner, the mortgage doesn't have to be in the name of all the owners.

8. Owning properties through a limited company

One of the most commonly asked tax questions is whether holding properties in a limited company, rather than as an individual or partnership, will save tax. Unfortunately, there isn't a definitive answer as it depends on a large number of factors, such as your personal circumstances and how long you intend to hold the properties. Any future changes in legislation could also affect the decision.

8.1. WHAT IS A LIMITED COMPANY?

A company has a separate legal status to its owners. This means that if you use a company to buy a property, its name will appear on the title deeds rather than yours. The ownership of a company depends on who holds its shares (the shareholders). There only needs to be one shareholder, so you could hold the company's only share and be its sole owner. Alternatively, all of your family could have a share in the company.

A company must also have at least one director and one secretary who can't be the same person. However, a director can also be a secretary as long as you've got someone else as a director as well. Usually, the main shareholder would be the director and a spouse or partner would be the company secretary.

Tɪᴘ. If you can't find anyone to be your company secretary, then, for a fee (around £200 a year), there are businesses who will do it for you. A web search for "company secretary service" will bring up several options.

8.1.1. Why is it called a limited company?

One of the non-tax advantages of having a company is that the owners are protected should a claim be made against it. For example, if one of your tenants falls down a step in your property and seriously hurts himself, he may decide to sue you. If you own the property, you would be personally liable to pay any damages awarded and could end up losing your own house. If the company owns the property, then you will have financial protection against any such claims. Your liability as a shareholder is, therefore, limited (hence "limited company") to the money you put into the company.

However, this doesn't mean that if the company takes out a large mortgage to buy a property and there's subsequently a crash in property prices, you can just walk away from the company's debts. This is because banks and other mortgage lenders are very cautious about lending to limited companies and will almost certainly require a personal guarantee from you as the owner. A personal guarantee means that if the company can't pay its mortgage debt, then the bank will come knocking on your door to settle up.

8.1.2. How do I set up a limited company?

First, you need to choose a suitable name for a company. You can't have the same name as another company (you can check whether your name is original by visiting the free "Webcheck" company information service on the Companies House website at http://www.companieshouse.gov.uk).

Once you have chosen a name, you also need to choose the director (most probably you) and the company secretary (usually a relative or friend).

The easiest way to legally set up a company is to use a formation agent. A web search for "company formation agent" will give a plethora of options.

A basic company formation can now be done within a day and will cost around £50 + VAT.

Alternatively, most accountants will be happy to set the company up for you (but their charges are usually higher).

Once the company is set up, you need to set up a company bank account. Certain banks offer free banking for companies with a relatively small number of transactions so shop around and don't automatically set up the account with the bank you use personally.

8.1.3. How much does it cost to run a limited company?

A company needs to pay an annual fee of £30 to Companies House (or £15 if you file the company's annual return online).

It also needs to file statutory accounts with Companies House and it's advisable to get an accountant to prepare these. The fee charged depends on the accountant, but for a simple property investment company with two or three properties, it should be in the region of £500-£750 plus VAT a year.

8.2. HOW IS RENTAL INCOME TAXED IN A LIMITED COMPANY?

Instead of income tax, limited companies pay Corporation Tax (CT) on their profits. The rate of tax they pay depends on their level of profits:

YEAR TO 31 MARCH PROFITS	2007 TAX RATE	2008 TAX RATE
Up to £300,000	19%	20%
£300,001 to £1,500,000	32.75%	32.50%
Above £1,500,000	30%	30%

These lower tax rates are the main reason that investors consider owning properties through a limited company. A higher rate taxpayer would pay 40% on their net rental income and gains. For companies with income and gains under £300,000 a year, the top company tax rate is only 20%.

Example

Jack, a higher rate taxpayer, has rental income of £9,000 a year. If he owned the property personally, he would pay £3,600 in tax on these profits. However, if the property was owned by a limited company, the company would pay tax of £1,800. A very significant tax saving of £1,800 on a relatively modest rental income.

NOTE. There may be further tax to pay if the profits are taken out of the company as dividends.

8.3. HOW ARE CAPITAL GAINS TAXED IN A LIMITED COMPANY?

Unlike sole owners and partnerships, a company doesn't pay CGT on any capital gains it makes on the sale of a property - it pays CT instead. Any capital gains are added to the company's rental profits in the year and the company then pays CT at the rates shown in 8.2.

Example

William purchased his property using a limited company. There was a taxable gain of £50,000 when the property was sold several years later.

The company also had rental income of £4,000 in the year the property was sold. So, the company will pay CT on total profits of £54,000. At this level, the rate of tax is 20%, and the company's tax bill will be £10,800 (20% x £54,000).

8.3.1. Can companies claim taper relief on their gains?

Unfortunately not. Taper relief can only be claimed by individuals. However, a company can claim indexation relief (see 4.3.) up to the date the property is sold (indexation relief was stopped for individuals in April 1998).

The indexation factors for companies from April 1998 can be found at http://www.hmrc.gov.uk/rates/c_gains_subject_c_tax.htm.

8.4. HOW DO I TAKE MONEY OUT OF A LIMITED COMPANY?

The company tax rates do seem very favourable compared with the higher income tax rate of 40% for all gains over £34,600 for 2007/8. However, you need to bear in mind that the profits must remain in the company to take full advantage of the lower CT rates. If you want to draw money out of the company, you will usually have to pay tax on this at the higher income tax rates. The two most common ways of taking money out of a company are as salary or dividends.

8.4.1. Paying yourself a salary

If you decide to draw money out of the company by paying a salary, then you will have to pay income tax on this. Both you and the company will also have to pay 12.8% National Insurance if the salary is more than £100 a week (2007/8).

Example

Neville needs to withdraw money from his property investment company. He decides to pay himself a salary of £4,000. As Neville receives a large salary from his main job, he will be taxed at 40% on this salary (£1,600). Therefore, he will only receive a net salary of £2,400. He won't have to pay National Insurance because the salary is less than £100 per week (£5,225 a year).

The company will also avoid paying 12.8% National Insurance as long as the salary is less than £100 per week. The salary can be offset against the company's profits to reduce its CT bill.

8.4.2. Paying yourself a dividend

One of the most popular methods of taking money out of a company is as a dividend. This is mainly because by paying a dividend, both you and the company avoid paying National Insurance.

The additional advantage is that a dividend carries a tax credit which means that basic rate taxpayers have no additional tax to pay. However, higher rate taxpayers still have to pay an additional tax equal to 25% of the dividend they receive.

The disadvantage of dividends is that the company cannot offset them against its profits to reduce the tax bill.

Example

Instead of a £4,000 salary, Neville decides to take the money out of the company as a dividend. In this case, Neville will pay tax of £1,000 (25% of £4,000) on the dividend. He therefore saves £600 by taking a dividend instead of a salary.

However, the company will lose CT relief on the £4,000, which at the small companies rate of 20% would mean additional CT to pay of £800. So overall, paying a dividend would mean paying an extra £200 in tax.

8.4.3. When is it preferable to take a salary?

Most tax advisers recommend that their clients take dividends rather than salary. However, there are times (as seen in the above example) when it's preferable to take a salary instead.

It would be preferable for you to take salary instead of dividends if:

- you are a higher rate taxpayer

- you want to withdraw less than £100 per week (£5,225 per year)

- the company has to pay tax at 20% or more.

Example

Michael is a higher rate taxpayer and wants to take £4,000 out of the company. If he takes the £4,000 as a dividend, he will have to pay 25% of the dividend in tax (£1,000).

If Michael takes the £4,000 as salary instead, he will have to pay 40% tax on this (£1,600). However, the company will be able to claim tax relief of 20% of £4,000 (£800). The overall tax cost is therefore £800 - a saving of £200 over the dividend.

It would also be very beneficial to pay a salary to someone who doesn't currently have any income (for example, your spouse or child). This is because the salary can be deducted from the company's profits to reduce the CT bill, but the individual won't pay any income tax or National Insurance.

Example

Brian pays his non-working wife a salary of £5,000 as she does occasional work for the company. As this is below the personal allowance of £5,225 (2007/8), his wife has no tax to pay. The company can still offset this salary against its profits, saving CT of £1,000.

8.4.4. When is it preferable to take a dividend?

If you're a basic rate taxpayer, it would be better to take a dividend than a salary.

Example

Anthony is a basic rate taxpayer and wants to take £4,000 out of the company. If he takes the £4,000 as salary, then he will pay £880 in income tax but the company will save £800 in CT. A net tax payment of £80.

However, if Anthony decides to take a dividend instead, he will have no additional tax to pay (he's a basic rate taxpayer) but the company will lose the £800 tax relief. Overall, a saving of £80 over paying a salary.

If you're a higher rate taxpayer and you want to withdraw more than £5,035 a year, the company will have to pay 12.8% National Insurance on any salary amount over this limit. In this case, it would always be better to take anything over £97 a week as a dividend.

8.5. ADVANTAGES OF USING A LIMITED COMPANY

As mentioned in 8.2., the main reason that property investors are buying properties through limited companies is the lower tax rates. However, there are other advantages to using a limited company.

Indexation relief

Unlike individuals, a company can claim indexation relief after April 1998. This relief increases the purchase cost in line with inflation, therefore reducing the gain.

Stamp Duty Land Tax savings

If you buy shares in a property company, then you will only pay Stamp Duty at 0.5% rather than up to 4% when you purchase a property as an individual.

Limited liability

If the company manages to get a mortgage without your personal guarantee, then your personal assets will be protected should there be a property price crash.

8.6. DISADVANTAGES OF USING A LIMITED COMPANY

As discussed in 8.3., one of the main disadvantages of having a limited company is that there could be a further tax charge should you wish to extract any of the proceeds from the company. There are also other tax disadvantages:

No annual CGT allowance

Unlike sole traders and partnerships, companies cannot use the annual CGT allowance (£9,200 for 2007/8). This means that if you and your spouse jointly owned a property, you would lose out on a combined CGT allowance of £18,400 if the property was held in a company. At the 20% small company tax rate that's extra tax of £3,680.

No Principal Private Residence relief

You cannot claim Principal Private Residence relief or Private Letting Relief when the properties are held in a limited company. Chapter 5 showed how important these reliefs could be in reducing, or even eliminating, the capital gain.

No taper relief

You can't claim taper relief when you sell a property in a company. This relief is worth up to 40% of the gain. However, companies do continue to get indexation relief (unlike sole owners and partnerships when it stopped in April 1998) to reduce the capital gain. So this may, or may not, give less relief over the ten years.

CGT when you transfer a property into a limited company

If you want to move a property into a limited company, then it must be transferred at market value. If the market value is more than what you originally paid for the property, then this could trigger an immediate CGT liability.

8.7. SO SHOULD I BUY A RESIDENTIAL PROPERTY THROUGH A LIMITED COMPANY?

The decision as to whether to own a property through a limited company depends on a number of factors:

- do you already run your business through your own company?

- how many similar properties do you want to purchase in the future?

- when do you intend to sell the property?

8.7.1. I already have a company

If you already run your business through a company it's normally more tax efficient to own the property personally.

This will enable you to have the benefit of taper relief of up to 40% and the use of your CGT annual exemption (and your spouse's annual exemption if the property is jointly owned).

The net rental income generated will be taxed at your top rate of tax (i.e. 40% for a higher rate taxpayer), but if you have a large mortgage on the property, it's likely that your income tax bill will be relatively small.

There are also other factors to consider:

Loss of business asset taper relief

If you already have your own company and you want to use it to buy a residential property, then you may find that the company fails to qualify as a trading company. This will mean that you won't be able to claim business asset taper relief (see 9.2.) when you sell your shares in the company.

Associated company problems

If you form a new company to buy the residential property and you own more than 50% of the shares in each one, you may find that you end up with a higher CT bill on your trading company. This is because (unless you make more than £1,500,000 of taxable profits) the two companies will be regarded as being "associated". When two companies are associated, the CT thresholds are halved. This means that it is only the first £150,000 of each company's profits that would be taxed at 20%. Even if you control one company and your spouse controls the other, the companies will be considered to be associated.

8.7.2. I don't already have a company

Personal or joint ownership may still be the more appropriate route due to the CGT taper advantages. However, if you are likely to be reinvesting the company's profits (rather than drawing money out of the company) to buy more residential properties then it may be beneficial to set up a limited company.

> *Example*
>
> *Simone owns three properties in her own name and she receives rental income of £16,000 a year from these properties. As a higher rate taxpayer, Simone will pay £6,400 leaving her with a net £9,600 to invest in her next property.*
>
> *If Simone owned the same three properties in her limited company, Simone Properties Ltd, then the company would pay just £3,200 in tax. This would leave the company with £12,800 to invest in the next property. An extra £3,200.*

NOTE. Although you can reinvest the profits, it's likely that at some point you will want to withdraw money from the company. Whenever you do this, you will be liable to the double tax charge - the company paying CT on the profits and you paying income tax on either the salary or dividend (but see 8.7.3.)

8.7.3. The tax advantages of long-term investment

There are potential long-term advantages of owning residential property in a company which counteract the loss of taper relief. These methods only work if you intend to keep the properties for a number of years.

Continue to rent the properties in the company as a retirement fund

If you intend to keep the properties for many years, then you could consider the property investment company as a "retirement fund". If the properties are retained into retirement, it's likely that any initial financing of the purchase of the property has been paid off and there will be a strong income stream. The profits of the company (after paying CT) can be paid out to you and/or your spouse as shareholder dividends.

To the extent that the dividends when added to your other income do not exceed your personal allowances and the starting and basic rate bands (£39,825 for 2007/8), you will have no income tax to pay.

Sell the properties and use the company as a retirement fund

This scheme works as long as you are happy to leave the rental income in the company to accumulate for a number of years.

As you know, if the rental income in your company is less than £300,000 a year then there is just 20% tax to pay as long as you don't take the income out as dividends. So, the after-tax rental profits are kept in the company until you wish to retire in, say, ten years' time.

Just before your retirement, you sell all the properties in the company. This will only trigger a CGT liability if the property values have increased by more than inflation.

You now need to get the money out of the company. If you wind it up to extract the funds as a capital distribution, then you'll have quite a large CGT bill (investment companies are only entitled to non-business asset taper relief, with the maximum being 40%).

However, you could take dividends instead (keeping your total income under £39,825) without paying any tax. Once you've taken most of the profits out as dividends, you can leave up to £15,333 (based on 2007/8 tax rates) in the company to cover the 40% taper relief and your CGT annual allowance), you can liquidate it without paying CGT.

By doing this, you have paid just 20% on your rental profits and avoided any tax on taking the money out of the company.

<u>Selling the shares instead of the property</u>

The advantages of taper relief can still be achieved if you sell the shares in the property investment company (after ten years of ownership) rather than the properties.

This may also be more attractive to the purchaser of the properties rather than buying the properties directly, as they will only have 0.5% Stamp Duty Land Tax to pay rather than the potentially higher sums (1% to 4%) of Stamp Duty Land Tax on the property purchases.

8.8. USING A PROPERTY MANAGEMENT COMPANY

If you've decided that it's desirable to hold the properties personally, you could still make use of the lower company tax rates by using a property management company.

8.8.1. What is a property management company?

A property management company is one that is set up to manage your property portfolio. However, the properties are still owned by you personally and not the company. Effectively, the management company acts as a letting agent.

The company would provide the usual letting agent services such as ongoing maintenance, repairs and property inspections.

The company would be set up as in 8.1.2.

8.8.2. How will a property management company save me tax?

As mentioned in 8.2., companies pay a lower rate of tax than individuals. The tax savings are best shown by way of example:

> *Example*
>
> *Lucy has a salary of £40,000 per year making her a higher rate taxpayer. She also owns three properties which give her rental profits of £7,500 a year. Therefore, she pays £3,000 (40% of £7,500) in tax on the rental profits.*
>
> *Lucy decides to set up a property management company to manage the properties. The company charges Lucy £625 per month to manage the properties. This means that Lucy is paying the £7,500 a year rental profits into the company as management fees.*
>
> *Lucy can deduct these management fees from her rental profits so her rental profits are reduced to nil and she has no tax bill. The company has tax to pay at 20% on its profits, i.e. £1,500 (£7,500 x 20%). Lucy, therefore, makes an overall tax saving of £1,500 a year.*

NOTE. If you already have a trading company and set up another company to act as the property management company, the two will be classed as associated and the 20% tax limit will be halved to £150,000 (see 8.7.1.) for each company.

8.8.3. How much can the property management company charge?

The charges must be at a commercial rate. If you only have one property, the Taxman won't let you get away with charging £625 a month. Commercial letting agents usually charge around 15% of the gross rental income for a full management service. Therefore, if you rent out a property for £600 a month, then the company can charge you £90 a month (15% of £600) as a management fee.

8.8.4. Does there need to be a formal contract between me and the company?

In order to avoid a challenge from the Taxman, yes. The contract should outline the management services that the company is providing to you such as:

- finding new tenants
- issuing tenancy agreements
- maintenance and upkeep of the properties
- resolving tenant queries.

The contract should also state the monthly charge (either as a fixed figure or as a percentage of the gross rental income).

See Appendix H for a sample contract.

8.8.5. Should I set up a property management company?

If you are a property investor and:

- you don't already have a limited company
- you are a higher rate taxpayer
- your rental profits are at least £2,500 a year.

then you will save tax by using a property management company. The rental profits should be above £2,500 in order that the tax saving (£500 for a higher rate taxpayer) is not wiped out by the additional cost of running a limited company (see 8.1.3.).

9. Investing in commercial property

9.1. WHY SHOULD I INVEST IN COMMERCIAL PROPERTY?

Most people choose to invest in residential properties such as houses and flats, which can be rented out relatively easily and provide excellent capital growth. However, investors are beginning to realise that commercial properties such as shops and offices can also provide a good return on the original investment (values are currently increasing by about 10% - 15% a year). Although, not as high as the recent massive hikes seen in the residential market, the commercial market tends to be more stable. Another big attraction is the high guaranteed rental income due to shops and offices usually being let on long leases, often ten to 15 years, compared with six months to a year for residential lets.

Shops and offices are also usually let on the basis that the tenant is responsible for repairs, renovations and insurance. So commercial property lets are often much easier to manage than residential ones.

Also, from a tax point of view, the current Capital Gains Tax (CGT) regime makes personal investment in commercial property much more favourable than investing in residential properties. One of the main reasons for this is the very generous business asset taper relief.

9.2. WHAT IS BUSINESS ASSET TAPER RELIEF?

The general principle of business asset taper relief is exactly the same as non-business asset taper relief (see 4.4.1.). However, the rates for business asset taper relief are much more valuable:

NUMBER OF COMPLETE YEARS OF OWNERSHIP	TAPER RELIEF (%)	EFFECTIVE RATE OF TAX FOR A HIGHER RATE TAXPAYER (%)	EFFECTIVE RATE OF TAX FOR A BASIC RATE TAXPAYER (%)
Less than 1 year	Nil	40	20
1	50	20	10
2	75	10	5

This means that if you're a higher rate taxpayer and hold a property qualifying as a business asset for more than two years, then you will effectively pay only 10% tax on any gain over the (current) £9,200 annual exemption.

Example

Tony bought a commercial property in April 2005 for £150,000. He decides to sell the property, which qualifies as a business asset, in May 2007 for £250,000. As a higher rate taxpayer, the £100,000 gain would give rise to a CGT bill of £40,000 without taper relief. As Tony has owned the property for more than two years, his CGT bill is just £10,000.

NOTE. Taper relief is only available to individuals and partnerships. It is not available to limited companies which own property.

TIP. To gain maximum taper relief, keep hold of the commercial property for a minimum of two complete years.

9.2.1. What types of property qualify as a business asset?

Unfortunately, not all types of commercial property qualify as business assets. The qualifying rules are quite complex and also depend on when you purchased the property and who is renting it.

Residential

Most residential property will not qualify as a business asset. However, the major exception to this is "furnished holiday accommodation" as long as certain criteria are met (see 3.2.).

Another exception is that if the property is let to a business (sole trader, partnership or unquoted trading company) and used as staff accommodation then it will also qualify as a business asset.

Finally, part of a residential property can qualify as a business asset if it is let to an individual who lives in it, but uses part of it for a trade purpose (such as storage of stock in the garage, working from home, etc.).

TIP. When selling a residential property, find out if your tenant used it as part of their business. If they have, make a partial claim for business asset taper relief to decrease the amount of CGT you have to pay.

Commercial

Since April 6, 2000, if you own a commercial property individually, it will qualify as a business asset if it is either used in your business or let to an "unquoted trading company" i.e. a limited company not listed on a stock exchange. If you let a property to a quoted trading company (i.e. listed on a stock exchange), it will only qualify as a business asset if you are a director or employee of the company (or own 5% of its voting rights).

However, from April 6, 2004, the definition of business assets has been extended to include commercial property let to unincorporated businesses, i.e. sole traders and partnerships.

So, unless you are letting to a quoted company, you do not need to be connected to the business letting the property. To summarise, you are entitled to claim business asset taper relief if:

- you personally own a property which is used by your business (whether you're a sole trader, partnership or limited company) or

- your (prospective) tenant is trading as an unquoted company or an unincorporated business (from April 2004). This includes an unquoted trading company using the property as staff accommodation.

9.2.2. Tax avoidance strategy: choosing the right type of tenant

As mentioned in 9.2.1., you can claim business asset taper relief even if you don't use the property in your own business and don't have any connection (other than as landlord and tenant) with the business renting the property.

However, you do need the right type of tenant in order to get the maximum 75% taper relief. Currently, the tenant needs to be either:

- an unquoted trading company or

- a sole trader or

- a trading partnership.

In all cases, the property must actually be used by the tenant in their trade.

If it's a quoted company (and you're not an employee of the company or own 5% of its voting rights) then the maximum taper relief would be 40% (giving an effective top CGT rate of 24%) and this would only be available after ten years of ownership.

> *Example*
>
> *Bette has been approached by both Tesco PLC and a local discount store, Savaquid Ltd, to rent her commercial property. Her rental income will be the same whichever she chooses, but there will be significant differences in the amount of tax she pays when she eventually sells the property:*

	SAVAQUID LTD	TESCO PLC
Taxable gain before taper relief	£150,000	£150,000
Less taper relief	£112,500	£60,000
Less annual allowance	£9,200	£9,200
Taxable gain	£28,300	£80,800
CGT to pay (40%)	£11,320	£32,320

By letting to the unquoted Savaquid Ltd rather than Tesco PLC, Bette will save £21,000 in CGT when she comes to sell the property.

If you're not sure whether a prospective tenant is quoted check at http://www.lse.co.uk/CompanyLookup.asp. Alternatively, you could just ask!

TIP. If you do want to let to a quoted company, you might want to consider getting a part-time job with them for, say, a few hours a week. As an employee, you'll be entitled to business asset taper relief. But you would have to keep the job for as long as you let to the quoted company so you don't lose any relief.

9.2.3. How do I calculate the relief where it's changed from a non-business to a business asset?

The full rate of business asset taper relief only applies if the property qualifies as a business asset throughout the entire period of ownership (starting April 6, 1998) or the previous ten years (whichever is the shorter). If it is a business asset for only part of this period then just that part of the gain attracts the business asset taper relief. The balance of the gain will attract the lower non-business asset taper relief. This is known as "tainted taper".

Consequently, for commercial property acquired before April 6, 2004 and let to an unincorporated business, the full 75% taper rate will not be available until April 6, 2014.

9.2.4. Tax avoidance strategy: untainting "tainted taper"

It is possible to obtain full business asset taper relief in less than ten years by triggering a new qualifying period of ownership. This can be done by transferring the property into a discretionary trust (see 6.3.5.) and holding over the capital gain. The transfer into a trust effectively starts a new period of ownership and after two years, maximum business asset taper relief can be obtained.

Example

Adam bought a commercial property in April 1998 and sold it in April 2006. It was let out to a sole trader business throughout his period of ownership. Therefore, it was classed as a non-business asset from April 1998 to April 2004 and as a business asset from April 2004 until April 2006. If Adam transfers the property into a trust in April 2004, he can hold over the gain and restart the taper clock - saving him a massive £20,250 in tax when he sells the property two years later:

	TAPER RELIEF	WITHOUT TRUST (£)	IN TRUST (£)
Sale proceeds		250,000	250,000
Less: cost		100,000	100,000
Gain		150,000	150,000
Taper relief			
£112,500*	@30%	33,750	
£37,500	@75%	28,125	
£150,000	@75%		112,500
Taxable gain		88,125	37,500
Tax at 40%		35,250	15,000

* This is the proportion of the total gain of £150,000 that is eligible for non-business asset taper relief (6/8ths of £150,000).

Conditions

Since December 10, 2003, any transfers you make into a discretionary trust will give rise to a potential CGT liability where you are still able to benefit from the trust. Therefore, you need to make sure that either;

- you put the property into a discretionary trust before you have a capital gain or

- other members of your family (such as your children), rather than you, are the trust beneficiaries.

So, this method will only really work if you are willing to give the property to someone else.

Warning!

Don't gift into a discretionary trust properties with a value exceeding £300,000 (for properties jointly-owned between spouses, it's £600,000). This is because lifetime Inheritance Tax is payable at 20% on transfers into a discretionary trust which exceed the nil-rate band (£300,000 for 2007/8).

9.3. SHOULD MY COMPANY'S PREMISES BE OWNED BY ME OR THE COMPANY?

Business asset taper relief is only available to individuals so it's almost always better to own your business premises personally and rent them to your trading company. In addition to being able to benefit from business asset taper relief, there are the following tax advantages:

- the rent you receive from your company allows profit to be extracted without having to pay National Insurance

- the rent is a tax-deductible expense for the company

- if you take out a mortgage on the property, you can offset the interest against the rent

- when you sell the property, you will receive the sale proceeds personally, therefore avoiding the double tax problem when trying to draw money out of a company.

9.3.1. What is a trading company?

As mentioned in 9.3., you can only claim business asset taper relief if you let the property to your trading company. The Taxman's definition of trading is most unhelpful:

> "A trade means a trade, profession or vocation conducted on a commercial basis with a view to realisation of profits."

So "trading" basically means selling goods and services to make a profit. However, the letting of property is not considered a trade. This means that if you let a property to your property management company (see 8.8.), you can't claim business asset taper relief when you sell that property.

Your company may hold some investments. This won't usually affect the trading status of your company as long as they form less than 20% of your company's activities.

9.3.2. Do I need a formal letting agreement between me and my company?

Yes, the rent should normally be paid under a formal agreement between you and the company. This agreement will set out how often the rent should be paid, either monthly, quarterly or annually. See Appendix I for a specimen licence agreement.

9.3.3. Tax avoidance strategy: use a licence instead of a lease

Problem

As discussed in more detail in 10.3., Stamp Duty Land Tax (SDLT) is due on the grant of a lease. The SDLT payable on the grant of a lease is based on the Net Present Value (i.e. the value in today's money) of all the rent payable under the lease over its full term. For commercial property, where the Net Present Value (NPV) is more than £150,000, SDLT is due at the rate of 1% on the excess. So if you decide to rent a property to your company, it would have to pay SDLT on any lease agreement with a net present value over £150,000 (visit http://www.hmrc.gov.uk/so/new-sdlt-calculators.htm to work out the net present value).

Example

Mr Austin owns a warehouse, which is occupied by his company, Austin Enterprises Ltd. Mr Austin wants to charge the company a rent so he can get money out of it without paying NI. If he grants the company a 20-year lease at an annual market rent of £30,000 per year, the adjusted NPV is £426,371 and SDLT of £2,763 is payable (£426,371 - £150,000 exempt = £276,371 x 1% SDLT rate).

If you let your company occupy your premises in return for a rent, the Taxman could argue that you have granted a lease even where there is no paperwork to prove that you have done so. If he treats it as a lease, then he could seek to collect the overdue SDLT plus interest and penalties.

Solution

One way that family companies can avoid SDLT is to use a licence to occupy instead of a lease. What's the difference? Put simply, a lease is a contract which gives the tenant exclusive possession for a period of time. On the other hand, a licence is a personal right to occupy property on a non-exclusive basis. The main differences are:

- a licence cannot be sold or given away whereas a lease can be assigned to someone else

- a lessor cannot enter the property whereas a licensor can.

Action

Speak to your solicitor and ask him to consider drawing up a licence instead of a lease.

9.3.4. How much rent should I charge?

A little?

You can charge the company as little rent as you wish for using your property. However, if the rent is not enough to cover the expenses connected with the property, such as loan interest, you will lose money. Any loss you make from letting property can only be offset against profits from letting in the future; it cannot be used to reduce tax due on your other income in the same or earlier years.

A lot?

If the company pays you a very high rent (above the market rate), the Taxman may argue that the excess is actually a disguised form of salary and will insist that this excess is taxed like a salary.

Ideally, you want to charge a rent that will just cover the property expenses, such as repairs, insurance and mortgage interest. Charging any more could mean that the rent is taxed at a higher rate in your hands than the profits would be taxed if they remained in the company. For example, the company may save Corporation Tax at 20% by paying you rent. You would then have to pay tax at your highest rate of 40% on any rent received that is not offset by the property expenses.

9.3.5. Do I have to charge VAT on the rent?

Not registered for VAT

You don't charge VAT on top of the rent you charge the company. However, you might end up with some irrecoverable input VAT suffered on the cost of acquiring the building originally and/or refurbishing it. The rule is, "no VAT charge, no VAT recovery!".

Registered for VAT

As the building is used for commercial purposes (i.e. not a residential property), you can register for VAT and opt to tax it. This means that you would charge VAT on the rent. However, you are now able to recover all the VAT on your costs. Of course, this means completing a VAT return and paying any VAT you owe.

9.3.6. So, should I register for VAT?

If you've been charged substantial VAT on acquiring the building or incur significant VAT on expenditure to it (e.g. during a refurbishment) then register for VAT and opt to tax and recover the VAT now. Assuming your company is also VAT-registered, it will be able to recover the VAT you charge it and you can also reclaim the VAT that you incurred.

If the company makes exempt supplies, then it won't be able to reclaim the VAT you would have to charge on the rent so it may be better for you not to register for VAT. However, if you had to pay a large amount of input VAT on the purchase of the property, then there will still be a cash-flow advantage in registering as you can claim all the VAT back on the purchase immediately.

If you haven't been charged VAT on acquiring the building and your VAT costs are small, then don't bother to opt to tax. The additional administration costs of completing quarterly VAT returns will outweigh any small VAT savings.

How do I opt to tax?

You can opt to tax by writing to HM Revenue & Customs and giving details of the property you want to opt. It's best to use form VAT 1614 which can be downloaded from http://www.hmrc.gov.uk. You need to notify HMRC within 30 days of opting.

TIP. It's important to establish that HMRC have received your notification to opt. Therefore, send in a duplicate notification for stamping and return by HMRC.

9.3.7. Tax avoidance strategy: register for VAT then de-register

Problem

You privately own a commercial property that you rent out. You have not exercised the option to tax because the property is occupied by a tenant (e.g. your company) which is either exempt or unregistered for VAT i.e. they could not reclaim any of the VAT you would have to charge on rent if you were registered. As you're not VAT registered, you can't reclaim the VAT on any major maintenance work done on the property.

Solution

Register for VAT and opt to tax the property. This way you can recover all of the input VAT on your major maintenance work. This must be done in advance of any work being started so that all the bills arrive after the VAT registration.

Once the work has been completed, de-register. You can voluntarily de-register because you are trading below the VAT limits (you no longer have to wait a year before de-registering).

Does the VATman really allow this?

On de-registration, you normally have to pay back the VAT on assets where the VAT comes to more than £1,000. However, this only applies to goods not services. Building work is classed as a service so is not caught by this provision.

NOTE. Even though you've de-registered for VAT, the option to tax will still apply for 20 years. This means that if you sell the building for more than the registration threshold during this period you will have to re-register for VAT. However, if there is a sitting tenant in the property, it should be treated as a "transfer of a going concern" and no VAT will be chargeable anyway.

9.4. TAX AVOIDANCE STRATEGY: USE A PENSION SCHEME TO BUY A PROPERTY

Rather than owning the property personally, you could set up a personal pension scheme which could own the property. The scheme could then lease the property back to your business.

The advantage of a pension scheme is that its income is tax-free so it wouldn't have to pay tax on the rent it receives from your company. Also, if you later sell the property in the pension scheme, you avoid paying CGT on any gain made.

Additionally, because all pensions are written in trust, your fund is not classed as part of your estate for Inheritance Tax purposes if you die before retirement.

9.4.1. How do I set up a pension scheme?

You need to speak to an Independent Financial Adviser (IFA) about your company setting up a Self-Invested Personal Pension (SIPP) and possibly transferring your current pension fund into it. A SIPP is basically the same as any other personal pension plan except that you have more control over what your contributions are invested in and one of the main attractions of a SIPP is that it can be used to purchase commercial property. This is enhanced by the fact that the Taxman will allow such a property to be leased back to your business. Therefore, you get a double benefit as the commercial property is being used both to help your business and provide for your future financial security.

Example

Tim has a company which is looking for new business premises. He has already accumulated £100,000 within his pension arrangements. A suitable property will cost £150,000. He has been advised that he could purchase a property by using a SIPP. The £100,000 already in his pension fund could be used as a deposit with the SIPP borrowing the remaining £150,000.

Tim's company would then be able to trade from the new property and pay a fair rent to the pension fund. The company will be able to offset this rent against its profits for tax purposes. The pension fund, however, would not have to pay tax on the rent or any capital gains should the property increase in value.

From Tim's point of view, although the property will assist him in building his business, it is also helping him build up his pension assets. Significantly, as the property is held within the pension fund, it would normally be creditor proof, should the company run into financial difficulties.

9.4.2. How much can a SIPP borrow to buy a commercial property?

Prior to "A" day (April 6, 2006), a SIPP could borrow up to 75% of a commercial property's purchase price. So, if your pension fund was worth £100,000, then you could have bought a property worth up to £400,000.

However, since April 2006, you are only able to borrow 50% of the fund's value. In this case, if your pension fund is worth £100,000, you can only buy a property worth up to £150,000.

9.4.3. What other benefits does a SIPP offer?

The flexibility of investment in a SIPP is not just limited to commercial property. You can also make direct investments in stocks and shares. This avoids you being locked into a poorly performing investment fund. As the SIPP enjoys all the tax advantages of an ordinary personal pension you can also switch to a new fund without paying any CGT.

9.4.4. What are the disadvantages of a SIPP?

The main disadvantage is centred around the fact that because a SIPP is a bespoke solution rather than an off-the-shelf product, the costs are higher.

9.4.5. Would I benefit from setting up a SIPP?

Due to the higher costs, you would only really benefit from a SIPP if you already have a reasonably large pension fund, say over £100,000, which you could transfer into it.

9.5. CAPITAL ALLOWANCES

The types of expenditure that you can claim against your commercial property rental income are much the same as for residential accommodation. The one major difference is that, unlike residential property (see 2.6.), if you own a commercial property (including furnished holiday accommodation), you can claim capital allowances on any fixtures and fittings that you purchase for use in the property. This compensates for the fact that you can't claim wear and tear allowance on commercial property rentals.

9.5.1. What are the capital allowance rates?

The rates for 2007/8 are the same as those shown in section 2.6. So, as a small business, you can claim 50% of the cost of a qualifying fixture or fitting in the first year (up until April 5, 2008) and 25% per year on the unrelieved balance thereafter.

9.5.2. Can I claim capital allowances on the fixtures present when I buy the property?

If you buy a commercial building – whether to trade from yourself or let out – you should be able to claim capital allowances on the plant and fixtures that are contained within it. But how do you put a value on these fixtures and fittings?

<u>Come to an agreement with the seller</u>

You can claim capital allowances on the fixtures and fittings in a commercial building, but usually you can't claim capital allowances on the building itself. So it's usually in your best interest to have as high a figure as possible allocated to fixtures and fittings. A higher value for fixtures and fittings could also save you Stamp Duty Land Tax (See 10.2.). If you and the seller so elect, you can decide between yourselves how much of the consideration is to be allocated to fixtures (but not moveable plant). By coming to an agreement, your respective local tax inspectors have no say in the matter. However, there are several conditions:

- the seller must have been claiming capital allowances on the fixtures

- both you and the seller must lodge a joint election with the Taxman showing how much consideration is to be allocated to the fixtures. The election must be made in writing within two years of the purchase and is irrevocable

- the value cannot exceed the original cost to the seller.

See Appendix J for sample wording for the joint election.

10. Other tax considerations when buying an investment property

10.1. SHOULD I TAKE OUT AN INTEREST-ONLY OR A REPAYMENT MORTGAGE?

As discussed in 2.2., any interest paid on a loan that is used exclusively for your rental property is tax deductible. However, the amount of tax relief you get depends on the type of loan you take out. Most property investors will finance the purchase of a property with either an interest-only or repayment mortgage. But which is the cheaper option?

Example

Repayment mortgage:

With a £100,000 property, on which you paid a deposit of £20,000, you have a ten-year repayment mortgage of £80,400 (that's £80,000 plus £400 for fees). Assuming a fixed rate of 6.35%, the interest cost in the first year would be £4,934.29 with capital repayments of £5,947.31, making a total payment of £10,881.60. In year two, the total payment is the same but the interest element has dropped to £4,545.45 and the repayment has increased to £6,336.15. This means less interest to claim against your rental income and so your tax bill increases by £155.54 (40% x (£4,934.29 -£4,545.45)). This may not seem like a lot but over the ten-year term adds up to about £9,000 in additional tax!

Interest-only mortgage:

If the same loan were on interest-only terms (i.e. no loan repayments), the annual interest cost would be the same over the ten years. In our example, that's £5,105.40 pa, a total of £51,054 over the life of the loan. This means £5,105.40 to deduct from your rental income each year. The difference in tax is shown in the table below.

Year	Repayment loan (£)	Interest-only loan (£)	Difference (£)	Tax saved at 40% (£)
1	4,934.29	5,105.40	171.11	68.44
2	4,545.45	5,105.40	559.95	223.98
3	4,131.18	5,105.40	974.22	389.69
4	4,689.83	5,105.40	1,415.57	566.23
5	3,219.63	5,105.40	1,885.77	754.31
6	2,718.68	5,105.40	2,386.72	954.69
7	2,184.98	5,105.40	2,920.42	1,168.17
8	1,616.38	5,105.40	3,489.02	1,395.61
9	1,010.61	5,105.40	4,094.79	1,637.92
10	364.78	5,105.40	4,740.62	1,896.25
Total	**28,415.81**	**51,054.00**	**22,638.19**	**9,055.29**

Table showing the difference in tax between an interest-only mortgage and a repayment mortgage.

As you can see, an interest-only mortgage means a lower tax bill. Also, although you may pay more interest with a repayment mortgage, the overall monthly payments are lower and you could use the additional funds to your advantage.

Tip. If you've got a mortgage on your own home then take out an interest-only loan to purchase a new rental property. Then out of the rents earned, re-direct the extra you would have paid on a repayment mortgage against your residential mortgage. This way you will pay less interest on your residential mortgage, which is not tax-deductible, and more interest on the buy-to-let mortgage, which is tax-deductible.

10.2. STAMP DUTY LAND TAX (SDLT)

From December 1, 2003, you have to pay Stamp Duty Land Tax (SDLT) when you purchase a property over a certain price threshold. The new tax is similar to the old Stamp Duty although there are some new rules for payment. SDLT is calculated as a percentage of the purchase price of the property and is paid by the purchaser.

10.2.1. Do I still have to pay SDLT if I'm not resident in the UK?

Unfortunately, yes. SDLT is payable whether or not the purchaser (or seller) is resident in the UK.

10.2.2. What are the rates of SDLT?

From March 23, 2006, the rates are:

Purchase Price	Stamp Duty
Residential property up to £125,000*	0%
Commercial property up to £150,000	0%
Residential property from £125,001 to £250,000	1%
Commercial property from £150,001 to £250,000	1%
All property from £250,001 to £500,000	3%
All property over £500,000	4%

* £150,000 if in a disadvantaged area.

The rate of SDLT remains the same whether you are an individual, partnership, company or trust.

As you can see, a small difference in the purchase price can make a huge difference to the amount of SDLT you pay.

Example

Paul wants to make an offer on a property of £251,000. If he purchases the property at this price then the SDLT rate on this property will be 3% and he will therefore have to pay an additional £7,530.

If, however, Paul offers £250,000 for the property, he will only pay SDLT at 1%, which would be £2,500.

In this case, a purchase price difference of £1,000, gives rise to an additional £5,030 in SDLT.

10.2.3. SDLT avoidance strategy: pay separately for fixtures and fittings

As we've seen, once the price passes the £250,000 threshold, the amount of SDLT due jumps from 1% to 3%, so it doesn't take mathematical genius to work out that you'd be better off buying at or below £250,000.

The seller, on the other hand, doesn't have to pay SDLT, so will want to get as much as possible for his property.

The solution would be for both you and the seller to come to an agreement whereby the seller prices the property at or below £250,000 and you pay separately for any furnishings or fittings.

Example

Andy wishes to purchase a house for £255,000. He offers the vendor £250,000 for the house and £5,000 for the carpets, curtains, light fittings, fitted oven, fridge and washing machine. The SDLT he has

*to pay will be £2,500. If he hadn't paid for the furnishings and fittings
separately he would have paid £7,650. He has therefore saved himself
£5,150 in SDLT.*

Pricing below the £250,000 threshold is, of course, legal, as is negotiating
a deal with the seller for furnishings and fittings that takes the actual price
paid above £250,000.

However, one of the differences between SDLT and the old stamp duty is
that buyers now face the possibility of an enquiry from the Taxman. This
is particularly likely when buying properties at a threshold (known as a
"pinch point") where the higher rates of tax apply. If you're in these zones,
make sure you can back up any separate figure you paid for furnishings
and fittings. The amount you pay for furnishings and fittings should be
a reasonable market value. If you've paid well over the odds, then the
Taxman may well question it.

What counts as furnishings and fittings?

As a rough guide, anything moveable is generally not considered to be
part of the property, and so is not subject to SDLT.

So, if you paid extra for plants in pots, that would be outside SDLT.
However, if they were planted in the ground, they would not be moveable
and would therefore be considered part of the property.

You could also pay separately for carpets, curtains, light fittings, fridges,
washing machines, garden furniture and ornaments.

10.2.4. How do I pay the SDLT?

You pay the SDLT to your solicitor who then forwards it on to the Taxman.
Although it's ultimately your responsibility, your solicitor will also complete
the self-assessment land transaction return for you (although you have
to sign it). This has to be submitted to the Taxman within 30 days of the
completion date and you, not your solicitor, will be liable to a £100 fine if
it's late.

10.2.5. So how else can I avoid paying SDLT?

Unfortunately, this is not an easy tax to avoid. However, properties in
certain areas of the country are exempt from SDLT.

In these so-called "disadvantaged" areas, the exemption relates to
residential properties purchased for less than £150,000.

Which areas are exempt?

There is an interactive disadvantaged area search tool on the Taxman's website, http://www.hmrc.gov.uk/so/dar/dar-search.htm. Just enter the postcode of the property you wish to buy and it will tell you whether it's a deprived area or not. You may be surprised by the areas that are classed as deprived - even parts of Kensington and Chelsea qualify!

WARNING! On his website, the Taxman has relied on postcode data for identifying exempt areas. But there is a time lag between a new postcode being created - for example, when a new development is built - and it being included on the Taxman's website. An estimated 8,000 new postcodes are generated in the UK every year. So, by relying on the website, you could pay SDLT when you don't need to.

As an alternative to the postcode search, you can download a list of all the SDLT disadvantaged areas from the following addresses:

COUNTRY	WEB ADDRESS
England	http://www.hmrc.gov.uk/so/dar/england.pdf
Wales	http://www.hmrc.gov.uk/so/dar/wales.pdf
Scotland	http://www.hmrc.gov.uk/so/dar/scotland.pdf
Northern Ireland	http://www.hmrc.gov.uk/so/dar/nireland.pdf

TIP. If you've bought a property in a disadvantaged area then make sure you haven't paid SDLT by mistake. It may have been missed by your solicitor and the Taxman won't automatically tell you it's exempt. If you find that have paid SDLT by mistake, then ring the Taxman's helpline (0845 6030135) for advice on how to reclaim it.

10.3. SDLT ON LEASES

As a property investor, you might think that this isn't particularly relevant to you. However, if you purchase a commercial property personally and then lease it to your company (see 9.3.3.), your company could end up paying SDLT on the lease.

10.3.1. How is SDLT calculated on the grant of a lease?

SDLT is based on the Net Present Value (i.e. the value in today's money) of all the rent payable under the lease over its full term.

If the Net Present Value (NPV) is less than £125,000 for residential properties or less than £150,000 for commercial properties, then there will be no SDLT to pay.

If the NPV is greater than £125,000 for residential properties or £150,000 for commercial properties, the rate of SDLT is 1% on the excess.

If you have exercised the option to tax on your commercial property (see 9.3.6.), then you also need to include the VAT as part of the rent payable.

10.3.2. How do I calculate the NPV over the term of the lease?

The NPV is the total rent payable over the life of the lease, reduced by an annual discount rate of 3.5% (to take account of inflation). Hence, the NPV of £10,000 due in twelve months' time is £9,662 (£10,000 divided by 103.5%).

Visit http://www.hmrc.gov.uk/so/new-sdlt-calculators.htm to calculate the NPV of the lease and the SDLT payable.

10.3.3. How can I avoid paying SDLT on leases?

One way of doing this would be to issue a licence instead of a lease - see 9.2.3. for details.

Section IV

Overseas property tax issues

11. Moving overseas

11.1. CAN I AVOID TAX BY MOVING OVERSEAS?

Moving abroad and becoming a tax exile is often thought as the ultimate tax avoidance scheme. So can it really work?

You can avoid UK Capital Gains Tax (CGT) on the sale of your UK properties by becoming non-resident here and satisfying the "five year rule" (see 11.1.3.).

NOTE. The UK includes England, Scotland, Northern Ireland and Wales. It does not include the Republic of Ireland, the Channel Islands or the Isle of Man.

To avoid UK CGT, you must not sell the property until the tax year following the one in which you left the UK. So, if you left the UK in the 2007/8 tax year, you could not sell the property until after April 6, 2008. If you sell it after you've left the UK, but before the end of the tax year, you will automatically have to pay UK CGT.

11.1.1. How can I become non-resident?

You normally stop being a UK resident from the day after your departure if either:

- you leave for full-time employment abroad for at least a complete tax year (the year that starts on April 6) - provided you spend less than 183 days in the UK in any tax year and your visits to the UK average less than 91 days a tax year, taken over a maximum of four tax years or

- you leave the UK permanently.

11.1.2. What does leaving the UK permanently actually mean?

To start with, unless you've got a contract to work abroad, you need to leave the UK for an entire tax year. In other words, to be non-resident for CGT purposes, you will have to leave the UK before, say, April 5, 2008 and not return until after April 6, 2009. You will also need to provide evidence of leaving the UK permanently.

Such evidence would be:

- buying a property abroad

- selling or letting out your UK property

- arranging for all your belongings to be transported abroad.

If you can't provide enough evidence at the start of your absence from the UK, then you will provisionally be treated as remaining resident in the UK for a period of up to three years. If, after three years, your UK visits have averaged less than 91 days a year, the Taxman will agree that you were not resident from the date you left the UK.

To summarise, as long as you don't spend more than 90 days a year in the UK after you've left, you will normally be treated as non-resident.

TIP. Once you leave the UK, make sure your trips back don't last more than seven weeks per tax year (April 6 to April 5). Keep your travel documents as proof of your arrival and departure dates.

11.1.3. Do I have to tell the Taxman I'm leaving the UK?

There's no longer a legal requirement to inform the Taxman of your departure from the UK. However, it's still a good idea to complete the form P85 (available at http://www.hmrc.gov.uk) explaining where you have gone and how long you expect to be away.

By doing this, the Taxman can't penalise you for not telling him your intentions.

You will also need to complete the "non-residence" pages on your self-assessment tax return.

11.1.4. What is the "five year rule"?

If you sell a property that you owned when you lived in the UK, then you won't be liable to UK CGT as long as you stay non-resident for five full tax years. This means that if you leave the UK before April 5, 2008, the earliest you could return would be April 6, 2013.

NOTE. You can still sell the property within five years of leaving the UK as long as you make sure you stay non-resident for five years. After that you can return to the UK and there will be no tax to pay.

Example

Mark and Val bought an investment property in the UK for £100,000 in October 2002. In July 2003, they emigrated to Spain. A year later, they decided to sell their investment property in the UK for £250,000.

Both being higher rate taxpayers, their potential Capital Gains Tax bill is £53,440. However, if they stay non-resident in the UK until April 6, 2009 (five complete tax years from the date they emigrated) they will have no UK CGT liability.

11.1.5. What happens if I sell my UK property and then return to the UK within five years?

If you sell your property while you are non-resident, but you return to the UK within five years, you will have to pay CGT on the sale of the property in the tax year that you return.

11.1.6. Can the five-year period be reduced?

Before March 16, 2005, the five-year period could be considerably reduced if you moved to a country which has a favourable double tax agreement (also known as a double tax treaty) with the UK. These agreements were set up to prevent people from paying tax twice (i.e. in two countries). They usually override UK tax legislation such as the five-year rule, and will often provide that any capital gain will only be taxable in the country where the individual is resident.

However, since March 16, 2005, anti-avoidance legislation has been introduced which means that individuals are no longer able to exploit the terms of any Double Taxation Agreement (DTA) to escape UK CGT.

So, if you've planning to become non-resident, be aware that you will still have to pay CGT if you return to the UK within five years.

11.1.7. Does the "five year rule" apply to any gain made on my main home?

Your main residence is exempt from UK CGT for up to three years after you move out (see 5.1.4.). The five year rule about not returning is therefore not an issue if you sell it within three years.

11.1.8. Will I have to pay CGT in my country of residence?

It wouldn't be much good avoiding UK CGT only to find that you end up paying more tax in your country of residence. So, before you move abroad, you need to find out whether gains on UK property are subject to tax in your proposed country of residence. You also need to check whether these local laws are overridden by the double tax agreement between the UK and your country of residence.

For example, under Spanish domestic law, if you are a Spanish tax resident you are liable to Spanish CGT on a sale of property anywhere in the world. However, this is overridden by (Article 13(1) and Article 24(4) of) the UK-Spain double tax agreement, which states that the country in which the properties are situated is the country which has the right to tax. So, the UK has the right to tax, but under UK domestic tax law, the UK does not tax because you will be non-UK resident. Therefore, you could avoid CGT altogether as long as you stay non-resident for at least five years.

As the CGT rules and rates in each country are different from those in the UK, and the double tax agreements can be quite complicated to interpret, we would advise you to seek advice from an international tax advisor.

TIP. Check the local tax rates on capital gains in the country where you are moving. For example, it wouldn't be worth avoiding UK tax at 40% if you then had to pay 55% tax on the gain because you were living in Belgium (Belgium's treaty with the UK does not protect gains on property in the UK).

11.1.9. Can I be resident nowhere and avoid CGT?

Yes, you can be resident nowhere. For example, you could take up residence on a yacht, sailing around sunnier climes, but not remaining in any one country (including territorial waters) for long enough to become resident in that country.

However, to avoid UK CGT on the sale of your UK properties, you would still need to follow the five year rule to prevent paying CGT on your return to the UK. So, it would have to be quite a long cruise!

11.2. CAN I ALSO AVOID INCOME TAX IF I'M NON-RESIDENT?

The rules for taxing income when you're overseas are quite different from the CGT rules. Even if you're no longer resident in the UK, you still have to pay UK tax on your rental income from any properties you own in the UK. This is often deducted at source under the "Non-Resident Landlords Scheme".

However, the personal allowance is usually available in such circumstances so you can still avoid paying tax on your UK rental income if your total UK income is less than £5,225 (2007/8).

11.2.1. What is the "Non-Resident Landlords Scheme"?

As its name suggests, the "Non-Resident Landlords Scheme" is a scheme for taxing the UK rental income of property investors who are not resident in the UK. However, just to be confusing, in this case you will be non-resident if you have been absent from the UK for just six months or more.

The scheme requires UK letting agents to deduct income tax at the basic rate (22% for 2007/8) from any rent collected for non-resident landlords. If you don't have a UK letting agent acting for you, or if a "let-only" service is provided, and the rent is more than £100 a week, then it is your tenant who must deduct the tax.

11.2.2. Can I apply to have my rent received without deduction of tax?

If you are a non-resident landlord and want to receive your UK rents without tax deducted, then you must apply for the Taxman's approval. If successful, a notice of approval will be sent to you and your letting agent or tenant, authorising them to pay your rent without deducting tax. Please note that, even though rent may be paid with no tax deducted, you are still liable to UK tax and, therefore, your rental income must be included on your self-assessment tax return.

Due to the increased administration, most letting agents prefer non-resident landlords to apply for approval to pay rent without tax deducted and will often charge you more if you don't get approval.

To apply for your rents to be received gross, complete form NRL1 which can usually be obtained from your letting agent or by telephoning the HMRC's helpline on 0845 070 0040. You should then send your completed form to: HMRC, Centre for Non-Residents, Unit 364, St John's House, Merton Road, Bootle, Merseyside L69 9BB.

11.2.3. Why might my application be unsuccessful?

If you have a poor tax history then your application may be declined. So, before applying, make sure all your tax affairs are up-to-date. Also, note that the Taxman can withdraw his approval if your self-assessment tax return is filed late or you don't pay any tax due on time.

12. Investing in overseas property

12.1. WHY INVEST IN OVERSEAS PROPERTY?

UK property investors are increasingly turning their attentions to buying property overseas where there is much faster capital growth so they can make a greater return on their investment. Investing in an overseas property can also provide a regular holiday home to enjoy and possibly even a place in the sun to retire to.

So, if you've decided to invest in an overseas property, what are the tax implications?

12.2. HOW IS OVERSEAS RENTAL INCOME TAXED?

If you are a UK resident and own an overseas property that you let out, then your rental profits are normally calculated in much the same way as UK property rental income. Unfortunately, however, the furnished holiday home rules never apply to overseas property even if you let it as a holiday home and satisfy the other criteria (see 3.2.1.).

However, if you are resident in the UK, but not UK domiciled, you will only pay income tax on your overseas rental income as and when the income is moved to your UK bank account (known as the "remittance basis").

12.2.1. Can I change domicile and avoid UK income tax by keeping the income overseas?

Domicile is different from nationality and residence and you can only have one domicile at a time. You are domiciled in the country that is your permanent home even though you may be working and living in another. You normally acquire the same domicile as your father when you are born. So, if your father's permanent place of residence was the UK, you will be domiciled in the UK.

It is very difficult to change your domicile and it would require a permanent move away from your original place of domicile to a new country with the intention of staying there until the end of your days.

However, this works in your favour if you were originally from overseas and are now resident in the UK. Unless you've taken positive steps to change your domicile, you will still be considered domiciled in your country of origin. Therefore, you can avoid paying income tax on your overseas property as long as you keep the rental income out of the UK.

12.2.2. What exchange rate do I use?

When preparing your overseas property accounts, the rental income should be the sterling equivalent of the overseas amount at the date it arises. However, you can simplify the calculation by using an average exchange rate for the year. You can find these rates at http://www.hmrc.gov.uk/exrate/index.htm.

12.2.3. If I've got UK and overseas property, can I group all the income together?

No. You can group all your overseas income together, but it needs to be shown separately from your UK property income. If you own properties in separate overseas countries, then you should prepare individual profit and loss accounts for each country's income. This is because income from different countries may be taxed differently due to different double tax agreements.

12.2.4. Which expenses can I claim against my overseas rental income?

The rules for which expenses you can claim are the same as for UK property income (see 2.1.) i.e. they must be wholly and exclusively for the purposes of your property rental business.

Travelling expenses

A very common question is whether you can claim your flight and other travel costs to your foreign property against your rental income. Unfortunately, you will only be able to claim these expenses if the reason for your trip is exclusively for your property business. This is often very difficult to prove because the Taxman will automatically assume that you're on holiday. Even if a journey is partly for maintaining the property etc., he will deny the relief.

Example

Helen owns a property in Italy. She goes out there for two weeks, partly to do up the property and partly to have a holiday. None of Helen's travel costs will be allowable.

If you want to claim the travel costs, then you will need strong evidence to prove that your trip was purely business. For example, you had to spend three weeks re-decorating the property and any private benefit was purely incidental.

Mortgage interest

There are several ways of raising the cash to buy your overseas property. You could use the property you are buying as security and borrow the money from a foreign bank. Alternatively, you may decide to re-mortgage your UK home to provide the funds to buy abroad. Either way, you can still offset the interest against your overseas rental profits in the same way as you can for UK income (see 2.2.).

Wear and tear allowance

Just to clarify, you can still claim wear and tear allowance against your overseas income as long as the property is fully furnished (see 2.5.1.). The allowance is 10% of the gross rents after deducting any expenses that were borne by you that should normally be borne by a tenant. So, if you pay for any of the following services, they need to be deducted from your gross rental income before calculating the wear and tear allowance:

- cable TV subscription
- telephone rental
- electricity and gas
- cleaning and laundry
- consumables (light bulbs, washing up liquid, toilet rolls etc.)
- refuse collection charges.

12.2.5. What can I do with any loss I make on my overseas rental income?

If you've more than one overseas property, you can offset the loss you make on one against the profit you make on another in the same tax year.

If that still leaves you with a loss then you can only carry the loss forward and offset it against any future overseas rental profits.

12.2.6. Where on my tax return do I put the overseas rental income?

Although the income is from property, it doesn't go on the "Land and Property" pages. Instead, you need to complete page F4 of the "Foreign" pages. If this is the first year you have received foreign rental income, you can download the "Foreign" pages from http://www.hmrc.gov.uk/saemployees/fagsa106.shtml.

12.2.7. Will I also have to pay tax on the rental income in the country where the property is situated?

Yes, you will probably have to pay tax on the rental income in the overseas country. However, you are usually entitled to a credit against your UK tax for any tax that you've already paid in the foreign country. You will be able to get a tax credit if the overseas country has a "double tax agreement" with the UK (see 11.1.6.). So, for example, if you received £5,000 in rental profits from a property in France, then you may have to pay tax on this in France, but you can offset it against your UK tax bill. However, if the foreign tax paid is more than the UK tax due, then the amount you can offset is limited to the amount of UK tax i.e. you can't claim a refund for the additional foreign tax paid.

12.2.8. How do I pay the overseas tax?

You will usually have to complete a tax return in that country and you should therefore seek advice from a local accountant. Many countries will withhold tax from your gross rental income to make sure that you meet your tax liability in that country. This is equivalent to the UK's Non-resident Landlords Scheme (see 11.2.1.).

For example, in Portugal, a withholding tax of 15% will be deducted from your rental income either by the tenant or by a local agent.

12.2.9. Is the tax year the same as in the UK?

No. In most overseas countries the tax year is the same as a calendar year i.e. it runs from January 1 to December 31. Therefore, you may have to prepare two sets of rental accounts, one to complete your UK tax return and one for your tax return in the overseas country.

12.3. HOW ARE CAPITAL GAINS ON OVERSEAS PROPERTIES TAXED?

Unless you are intending to retire overseas, it is likely that at some point you will want to sell the property. Therefore, before buying a foreign property, it is important to consider the CGT implications. There would be no point making a significant capital gain only to see it wiped out by a hefty tax bill.

12.3.1. Is CGT due in the UK on an overseas property?

If you are a UK resident, you have to pay CGT on your worldwide property gains. However, if you are not domiciled in the UK, you can avoid paying CGT as long as you make sure the proceeds stay outside the UK.

12.3.2. How do I calculate the gain when it's in a foreign currency?

The gain is calculated in much the same way as a gain on UK property (see Chapter 4). The gain or loss on the disposal of property abroad is arrived at by comparing the sterling equivalent of the cost at the date of purchase with the sterling equivalent of the proceeds at the date of sale. Unfortunately, you can't take advantage of a favourable exchange rate by working out the gain in the foreign currency and then converting it.

12.3.3. Is CGT due in the overseas country?

Selling a property overseas will usually give rise to a gain in the overseas country as well as in the UK. However, if you had to pay tax in the foreign country, you would be able to offset it against your UK CGT bill.

The calculation for capital gains varies from country to country and you could find that the tax you have to pay in the foreign country is greater than the UK tax due. In this case, the amount of foreign tax you can deduct cannot be more than the UK CGT due and you would effectively be paying the tax rate on the gain in the foreign country.

However, as the table below shows, most countries have lower rates of CGT than the UK 40% rate.

	FRANCE	SPAIN	PORTUGAL	CYPRUS
CGT rate	16%	35%	25%	20%

12.4. WHAT ARE THE INHERITANCE TAX IMPLICATIONS OF OWNING OVERSEAS PROPERTY?

Inheritance Tax (IHT) is due on all your worldwide property as long as you are domiciled in the UK, or deemed UK domiciled for IHT purposes. Someone resident in the UK for at least 17 of the last 20 tax years is deemed UK domiciled for IHT purposes.

However, estate taxes are normally also due on property in the overseas country and it is usually the foreign country that has the first right to tax. Any foreign tax paid can then be offset against the UK IHT bill.

12.4.1. Forced heirship

You should not presume that a foreign country will recognise your UK will. In some countries, you cannot give your estate away as intended in your will as it is necessary to benefit particular family members. The state actually dictates who can inherit and how much.

France, Italy and Spain all have forced heirship rules and you should seek advice from a legal expert on ways of dealing with this.

12.5. SHOULD I SET UP A LIMITED COMPANY TO INVEST IN OVERSEAS PROPERTY?

There's no definitive answer to this question as it depends on the laws of the country you want to invest in and whether you want to rent it out permanently or occupy the property yourself some of the time.

Property investors set up limited companies for a variety of reasons. For example, to avoid local property taxes in Portugal or forced heirship rules in France. In other countries, local laws do not allow foreign individuals to buy property directly so you may have to set up a company to buy there e.g. Bulgaria. You should therefore seek advice from an expert in the foreign country's tax system before deciding whether you should set up a limited company.

In the past, if you decided to purchase an overseas property through a company, you had to take care to ensure that an unwelcome UK benefit-in-kind charge did not arise because you or your family also use the property as a holiday home.

However, the Taxman recently scrapped the tax charge as long as the company is owned by individuals, the property is the company's only asset and is used solely by the owner or his family as part of his domestic arrangements.

12.5.1. Can I avoid UK income tax if I set up an offshore company?

This party depends on where the company's management and control are but as a UK resident it will be virtually impossible to avoid tax by setting up an offshore company. If you control the company from the UK, then it will be considered to be a UK resident company. And if it's resident in the UK then it will be subject to UK tax rules.

UK resident company

If a UK resident company owns property abroad, it is liable to Corporation Tax on income received before deduction of foreign taxes, and also on any capital gains on the disposal of foreign properties. A company's income from all property let abroad is treated as the profits of an "overseas property business" and computed in broadly the same way as for individuals, but with the profit or loss computed separately for properties in different countries in order to calculate the amount of any available double tax relief.

Offshore company

Even if the company's management and control are outside the UK, it's likely that the Taxman will still try and tax the income. This is because he has special anti-avoidance provisions that prevent an individual (or his spouse) who is resident in the UK from obtaining a tax advantage by owning properties in an offshore company while he still benefits from the income.

However, these special rules do not apply where the offshore company is set up for genuine commercial reasons and not to avoid tax. Therefore, if you are considering investing in a country such as Bulgaria where you have to set up a company to buy property, then you have a strong argument for saying that the anti-avoidance provisions don't apply and that you shouldn't be taxed on the offshore company's income.

12.5.2. Can I avoid UK CGT if I set up an offshore company?

Special rules also apply to capital gains in offshore companies if the company would be considered a close company (i.e. it has less than five directors/shareholders) if it were a UK resident. A company owned by just you and your spouse would be a close company.

In such a case, you will be personally taxed on any capital gain in proportion to your shareholding in the company. So having an offshore company doesn't automatically mean you will avoid UK CGT.

12.6. ARE THERE ANY OTHER TAXES THAT I NEED TO CONSIDER?

You need to be fully aware of any other taxes that you may incur on foreign property and again you should seek advice from an expert. There are a raft of other taxes, but two common ones are:

Purchase taxes

Most countries will charge some sort of tax when you purchase a property. For example, in Spain it's 7% of the purchase value.

Wealth tax

Many countries (including France and Spain) charge annual local wealth taxes. These are usually calculated on the value of the property after any mortgage. You can reduce the charge significantly by borrowing against the overseas property

Section V

Appendices

APPENDIX A
CLAIMING RELIEF ON FURNISHED HOLIDAY HOME LOSSES

HM Revenue & Customs

. . . . *(insert address)*

. . . .

. . . .

. . . .

. . . . *(insert date)*

Your ref . . . . *(insert your ten digit tax reference)*

Dear Sirs

Furnished holiday home business losses

In the tax year ended April 5, ... *(insert year)*, my furnished holiday letting business made a loss of £ . . . . *(insert figure)*. In accordance with the provisions of s.380(1) Income and Corporation Taxes Act 1988, I wish this loss to be carried back and set against my general income for the tax year ended April 5, ... *(insert year)*.

Please could you acknowledge receipt of this claim.

Yours faithfully

. . . . *(insert name)*

APPENDIX B
INDEXATION ALLOWANCE

Individuals and others within the charge to Capital Gains Tax are not entitled to indexation allowance for any period after April 1998. To calculate indexation allowance up to April 1998, on disposals on or after 6 April 1998, use the table below.

You work out the indexation allowance by multiplying the amount you spent by the indexation factor.

Year	Jan	Feb	Mar	Apr	May	Jun	Jul	Aug	Sep	Oct	Nov	Dec
						Month						
1982			1.047	1.006	0.992	0.987	0.986	0.985	0.987	0.977	0.967	0.971
1983	0.968	0.96	0.956	0.929	0.921	0.917	0.906	0.898	0.889	0.883	0.876	0.871
1984	0.872	0.865	0.859	0.834	0.828	0.823	0.825	0.808	0.804	0.793	0.788	0.789
1985	0.783	0.769	0.752	0.716	0.708	0.704	0.707	0.703	0.704	0.701	0.695	0.693
1986	0.689	0.683	0.681	0.665	0.662	0.663	0.667	0.662	0.654	0.652	0.638	0.632
1987	0.626	0.62	0.616	0.597	0.596	0.596	0.597	0.593	0.588	0.58	0.573	0.574
1988	0.574	0.568	0.562	0.537	0.531	0.525	0.524	0.507	0.5	0.485	0.478	0.474
1989	0.465	0.454	0.448	0.423	0.414	0.409	0.408	0.404	0.395	0.384	0.372	0.369
1990	0.361	0.353	0.339	0.3	0.288	0.283	0.282	0.269	0.258	0.248	0.251	0.252
1991	0.249	0.242	0.237	0.222	0.218	0.213	0.215	0.213	0.208	0.204	0.199	0.198
1992	0.199	0.193	0.189	0.171	0.167	0.167	0.171	0.171	0.166	0.162	0.164	0.168
1993	0.179	0.171	0.167	0.156	0.152	0.153	0.156	0.151	0.146	0.147	0.148	0.146
1994	0.151	0.144	0.141	0.128	0.124	0.124	0.129	0.124	0.121	0.12	0.119	0.114
1995	0.114	0.107	0.102	0.091	0.087	0.085	0.091	0.085	0.08	0.085	0.085	0.079
1996	0.083	0.078	0.073	0.066	0.063	0.063	0.067	0.062	0.057	0.057	0.057	0.053
1997	0.053	0.049	0.046	0.04	0.036	0.032	0.032	0.026	0.021	0.019	0.019	0.016
1998	0.019	0.014	0.011									

APPENDIX C
CLAIMING EARLIER YEAR LOSSES ON SHARES

HM Revenue & Customs

. . . . *(insert address)*

. . . .

. . . .

. . . .

. . . . *(insert date)*

Your ref . . . . *(insert your ten digit tax reference)*

Dear Sirs

Amendment under s.33 Taxes Management Act 1970

In the tax year ended April 5, ... *(insert year)*, I sold . . . . *(insert figure)* shares in . . . . *(insert name)* plc for £ . . . . *(insert figure)*. This resulted in a capital loss of £ . . . . *(insert figure)*. In accordance with the provisions of s.33 TMA 1970, I would like to amend my . . . . *(insert year)* tax return to include this loss on the return.

Please could you acknowledge receipt of this claim.

Yours faithfully

. . . . *(insert name)*

APPENDIX D
NEGLIGIBLE VALUE CLAIM

HM Revenue & Customs

.... *(insert address)*

....

....

....

.... *(insert date)*

Your ref .... *(insert your ten digit tax reference)*

Dear Sirs

Negligible value claim

I claim relief under s.24(2) of the Taxation of Capital Gains Act 1992 for the tax year ended April 5, ... *(insert year)* in respect of my shareholding in .... *(insert company name)* plc which cost £ .... *(insert figure)*.

*[The shares are included on the "negligible value list" maintained by the Shares Valuation office and were of negligible value as at the date of this claim].

*[The shares are not currently included on the "negligible value list" maintained by the Shares Valuation office, but I believe the shares are of negligible value and would ask the Shares Valuation office to consider including them on the list].

Please could you acknowledge receipt of this claim.

Yours faithfully

.... *(insert name)*

*delete as appropriate

APPENDIX E
PRIVATE RESIDENCE ELECTION

HM Revenue & Customs

.... *(insert address)*
....
....
....
.... *(insert date)*

Your ref .... *(insert your ten digit tax reference)*

Dear Sirs

Private residence election

I acquired a second residence on .... *(insert purchase date)*. In accordance with the provisions of s.222(5) Taxation of Chargeable Gains Act 1992, I hereby elect that the following property should be treated as my main residence with effect from .... *(insert date)*.

.... *(insert address)*

....

....

....

Please could you acknowledge receipt of this election.

Yours faithfully

.... *(insert name)*

APPENDIX F
VARIATION OF PRIVATE RESIDENCE ELECTION

HM Revenue & Customs

. . . . *(insert address)*

. . . .

. . . .

. . . .

. . . . *(insert date)*

Your ref . . . . *(insert your ten digit tax reference)*

Dear Sirs

Variation of private residence election

I have currently elected that . . . . *(insert address)* should be treated as my main residence for Capital Gains Tax purposes. In accordance with the provisions of s.222(5) Taxation of Chargeable Gains Act 1992, I now wish . . . . *(insert address)* to be regarded as my main residence with effect from . . . . *(insert date)*.

Please could you acknowledge receipt of this election.

Yours faithfully

. . . .*(insert name)*

APPENDIX G
LETTER OF WISHES

LETTER OF WISHES

Dated . . . . *(insert date)*

To: The Trustees of my Will

By my Will, I have appointed you as my Trustees and have left you the whole or part of my estate to hold in Discretionary Trusts for the benefit of my wife/husband/partner* and family. My Will gives you wide powers not only in relation to the management of the assets of the Trust Fund, but also in relation to the timing and manner in which those assets are distributed.

This letter is not legally binding upon you. Circumstances may arise under which you consider, quite properly, that to follow strictly this letter of wishes would be inappropriate.

(1) During the lifetime of my wife/husband/civil partner*

Whilst my wife/husband/partner* is alive I wish you to regard her/him* as the principal beneficiary, ensuring so far as is possible that her/his* wishes are observed and her/his* welfare regarded as being of paramount importance. Subject to my wife's/husband's/partner's* wishes and welfare, I would want you to exercise your powers in such a way as will secure the least amount of tax being payable on my wife's/husband's/partner's* death.

(2) After the death of my wife/husband/partner*

After the death of the survivor of me and my wife/husband/partner*, I should like you to divide the Trust Fund equally between my children as and when they each attain the age of . . . . *(insert age).*

Once a child reaches . . . . *(insert age),* I would expect you to distribute her/his* share outright. However, there may be circumstances justifying the postponement of a distribution beyond the age of . . . . *(insert age),* for example, the child may be a party to an unstable marriage, may be embarking on a risky business venture or may wish her/his* share to be retained in Trust for the benefit of her/his* children, thereby mitigating the impact of Inheritance Tax, Income Tax or Capital Gains Tax.

Whilst any of my children are between the age of . . . . *(insert age range)*, I should be quite happy to see the income from their respective shares of the Trust Fund distributed to them.

(3) Death of child

If any of my children should fail to attain the age of . . . . *(insert age)*, but have children of their own, then I would expect that my deceased child's share would be retained on Trust for the benefit if her/her* children when they, in turn, reach . . . . *(insert age)* and the share treated much in the same way as their deceased parent's share (as mentioned above).

In the event of my wife/husband/partner* and all my children (and any children they may have) dying before the Trust Fund has been fully distributed, then I would expect you to distribute the Trust Fund as follows: . . . . *(insert details of how you would like the Trust Fund distributed)*.

I reserve the right to revoke or vary these wishes.

Signed: . . . .

Dated: . . . .

* delete as appropriate

APPENDIX H
PROPERTY MANAGEMENT COMPANY CONTRACT

CONTRACT FOR MANAGEMENT SERVICES

This agreement is made on .... *(insert date of agreement)* between

(1) .... *(insert property management company name)* (the "Company")
and

(2) .... *(insert property owner name)* (the "Property Owner")

FINDING TENANTS

The Company will find a suitable tenant for the Property Owner for a fee of .... *(insert figure)*. This fee must be paid upon commencement of the tenancy. The service will include: continuously and vigorously advertising your property until it has been let to a suitable tenant. Placing advertisements in newspapers. Interviewing and vetting all suitable prospective tenants and taking them to view the property. Taking up references from all tenants and supplying contracts.

ONGOING MANAGEMENT SERVICE

For .... *(insert figure)* of the rental payment over the period of the Tenancy Agreement, the Company will carry out the following services on behalf of the Property Owner:

- rent collection

- notification to service companies at the commencement of the tenancy e.g. gas, electric, water council tax

- arrangement and supervision of minor repairs to the property and general maintenance.

ADDITIONAL SERVICES

Inventory

The Company will charge a fee of. .... *(insert figure)* for preparing an inventory. This includes compiling and inventory for three bedrooms, two reception areas, kitchen and bedroom. For each additional room or out house there will be an extra charge of .... *(insert figure)*.

Renewal

If the original tenancy is extended for the same tenant or occupier, a further charge will become payable to the Company at the outset of such extended periods at the rate of . . . . *(insert figure)* of the rental payable during extended period.

Inspections

The Company will make quarterly inspections during the period of letting to ensure the premises are being use in an appropriate manner. The charge will be . . . . *(insert figure)* per inspection.

Signed on behalf of the Company . . . .

Name (in capitals) . . . .

Position . . . .

Signed by the Property Owner . . . .

Date . . . .

APPENDIX I
LICENCE

In respect of .... *(insert address)*

THIS LICENCE is made on ....*(insert date)*

Between

.... *(insert name)*, ("the Licensor") and

.... *(insert Company name)*, ("the Licensee")

The Licensor and the Licensee have agreed to occupation of the premises known as ....
.... *(insert property address)* on the following terms:

1. The licence to run for a term of .... *(insert term)* commencing on ....
    .... *(insert start date)* and expiring on .... *(insert finish date)*.
    At the end of the Licence the Licensee will offer vacant possession if a formal renewal has
    not been completed.

2. The Licence fee to be £ .... *(insert figure)* per month, payable in advance
    calendar monthly by standing order. This fee is exclusive of all non-domestic and water
    rates and all other outgoings and is payable from the .... *(insert start
    date)*.

3. The Licensor reserves the right to increase or decrease the licence fee at his discretion.
    The Licensor will give the Licensee reasonable written notice of any significant increase
    or decrease in the fees payable.

4. The Licensee to maintain and give up on termination of the Licence the interior of the
    premises in as good and substantial repair and decoration as exists before this Licence
    commences and the Licensee upon notice shall immediately attend to necessary repairs.

5. The Licensee to comply with any enactments or regulations or such like which may be
    required from any competent Authority.

6. The Premises are not to be used other than for normal .... *(insert
    office/manufacturing etc.)* purposes in connection with the Licensee's proposed business.
    The Licensee is not to do or permit anything to be done on the premises which is illegal.

7. The Licensee to insure and keep insured the premises against loss by fire and such other
    perils.

8. The Licensee to permit the Licensor at any reasonable time to enter the premises.

9. The Licensee to indemnify and keep indemnified the Licensor against all actions, claims and demands arising from the Licensee's use and occupation of the premises.

10. At any time within the term of the Licence, the Licensee or Licensor may give one calendar month's notice to terminate this Licence.

11. By signing this agreement, the Licensee formally acknowledges that this is a Licence only and no tenancy is created, whether formal or informal.

Signed for the Licensor:. . . . .

Name: . . . . *(insert your name)*

Date: . . . .

Signed for the Licensee: . . . .

Name: . . . . *(insert Company name)*

Date: . . . .

APPENDIX J
CAPITAL ALLOWANCES ELECTION

Notification of an Election to use an alternative apportionment in accordance with s.198 Capital Allowances Act 2001, Section 198 between .... *(insert name of seller)* and .... *(insert name of buyer)*.

Property address:

Interest *(freehold / leasehold):*

Seller's name and address:

Tax district and reference:

Buyer's name and address:

Tax district and reference:

Date of completion of sale:

Amount apportioned to machinery and plant fixtures (£):
(see attached for details)

Sale price *(£)*:

The seller and the buyer hereby jointly elect, pursuant to the provisions of s.198 Capital Allowances Act 2001, that the amount of the sale price to be treated as capital expenditure on plant and machinery incurred by the buyer on the provision of the fixtures is *(insert amount as above)*. A list of the fixtures is given on the next page.

Signed: ....

Name of seller: ....

Date:..

For and on behalf of .... *(insert name of the seller)*

Signed: . . . .

Name: . . . .

Date: . . . .

For and on behalf of . . . . *(insert name of the buyer)*

Example:

Schedule of Plant and Machinery to be included in s.198 Election

. . . . *(insert address)*

Item	Apportioned Amount
Ventilation	£4,500.00
Blinds	£1,500.00
Total	**£6,000.00**

CLAUSES FOR CONTRACT

1. Have any of the Fixtures included in the transaction been included in an election either under s.198 or s.199 Capital Allowances Act 2001 or s.59B of the Capital Allowances Act 1990? If so, please provide a copy of such election notice(s).

2. If requested by us, will you enter into an agreement with us to make an election under s.198 or s.199 of the Capital Allowances Act 2001?